מזמור לאלי
MIZMOR L'ELI

מנגינות-תפילה של אליהו שלייפר
ELIYAHU SCHLEIFER ANTHOLOGY

Edited by JOEL EGLASH and CANTOR ELIYAHU SCHLEIFER

Editorial committee:
CANTOR DAVID BERGER
CANTOR EVAN COHEN
JOEL EGLASH
CANTOR ROSS WOLMAN

TMP
TRANSCONTINENTAL
MUSIC PUBLICATIONS
A Division of the American Conference of Cantors

HEBREW PRONUNCIATION GUIDE

VOWELS	CONSONANTS
a as in father	ch as in Bach or Scottish loch (not as in cheese)
ai as in aisle (= long i as in island)	g = hard g as in get (not soft g as in gem)
e as in bed	tz as in boats
ei as in eight (= long a as in ace)	h after a vowel is silent
i as in pizza (= long e as in be)	r = like the Italian (rolled) or French r
o as in go	
u as in lunar	
' = unstressed vowel close to ə or unstressed short e	

MIZMOR L'ELI: ELIYAHU SCHLEIFER ANTHOLOGY

Proofread by Cantor David Berger, Cantor Evan Cohen, Cantor Claire Franco, and Cantor Ross Wolman
Copyedited by Debra Corman – Music engraved by Josh Wiczer
Cover and interior photographs (HUC–JIR, Jerusalem) by Michal Lev-Hamon – Design and compositing by Joel Eglash

Transcontinental Music Publications Executive Committee:
—Joel Eglash, Cantor Lauren Phillips Fogelman, Cantor Claire Franco, and Cantor Steven Weiss
American Conference of Cantors: President, Cantor Seth Warner; COO, Rachel Roth
TMP/JLicense Customer Support: Stacey Berliner – TMP/JLicense Production Assistant: Eden Franco

TRANSCONTINENTAL MUSIC PUBLICATIONS / JLICENSE
A DIVISION OF THE AMERICAN CONFERENCE OF CANTORS
The world's leading publisher of Jewish music since 1938
1375 Remington Road, Suite M – Schaumburg, IL 60173
847.781.7800 – tmp@accantors.org

Printed in the United States of America – 10 9 8 7 6 5 4 3 2 1
Item number 994058 – ISBN 979-8-9889024-3-0
Includes audio download code insert

TranscontinentalMusic.com

The anthology *Mizmor L'Eli* is dedicated with love

to my wife and partner, Aya Laipsker Schleifer

and to our two sons, Doron and Uri Schleifer

Transcontinental Music Publications and the American Conference of Cantors are grateful to these generous donors who made *Mizmor L'Eli* possible:

Cantor Jill Abramson
Cantor Lauren Adesnik
Cantor Joanna Alexander
Cantor Lisa Arbisser
Professor Merri Lovinger Arian
Cantor Matthew Austerklein
Cantor Devorah Avery
Cantor Donna Azu
Cantor Lauren Bandman
Cantor David Berger
Cantor Julie Berlin
Cantor Dr. Andrew Bernard
Cantor Rabbi Arlene Bernstein
Cantor Jennifer Bern-Vogel
Cantor Susan Bortnick
Cantor Rabbi Richard and Linda Botton
Cantor Joshua Breitzer
Cantor Ida Rae Cahana
Cantor Deborrah Cannizzaro
Cantor Susan Caro
Cantor Mark Childs
Aryell Cohen
Cantor Evan Cohen
Cantor Richard Cohn
Cantor Joel Colman
Cantor Lori Corrsin
Cantor Galit Dadoun Cohen
Cantor Lisa Doob
Cantor Ellen Dreskin
Cantor Nancy Dubin
Cantor Harriet Dunkerley
Cantor Kari Siegel Eglash and Joe Eglash
Cantor Miriam Eskenasy
Cantor Kenneth Feibush
Cantor Devorah Felder-Levy
Cantor Geoffrey Fine
Cantor Alisa Fineman
Cantor Lucy Fishbein
Cantor Tracy Fishbein
Cantor Joseph Flaxman
Cantor Lauren Phillips Fogelman
Cantor Claire Franco
Cantor Erin Frankel
Cantor Jordan Franzel
Cantor Jennifer Frost
Cantor Rebecca Garfein
Cantor Margot Goldberg
Cantor Marla Goldberg
Cantor Elizabeth Goldmann
Cantor Jonathan Grant
Cantor Orna Green
Cantor Rabbi Jon Haddon
Cantor Kim Harris
Cantor Rabbi Rhoda Harrison
Cantor Deborah Hartman
Cantor Kat Hastings
Cantor Naomi Hirsch
Hebrew Union College–Jewish Institute of Religion, New York Campus Faculty
Cantor Zöe Jacobs
Cantor Marcy Kadin
Cantor Rachel Kalmowitz
Cantor Patrice Kaplan
Cantor Nancy Kassel
Cantor Alane Katzew
Cantor Jason Kaufman
Cantor Evan Kent
Cantor Ilene Keys
Cantor Todd Kipnis
Cantor Jeffrey Klepper

Cantor Hayley Kobilinsky
Cantor Sharon Kohn
Cantor Leigh Korn
Cantor Alexandra Kurland
Cantor Allen Leider
Cantor Janet Leuchter
Cantor Lisa Levine
Cantor Martin Levson
Cantor Barbra Lieberstein
Cantor Arik Luck
Cantor Emma Lutz
Cantor Benjamin Maissner
Cantor Michael Mandel
Cantor Aviva Marer
Cantor Andrea Rae Markowicz
Rabbi Cantor Jacqueline Marx
Cantor Judith Meyersberg
Cantor Sydney Michaeli
Cantor Rebecca Moses
Cantor Daniel Mutlu
Cantor Shira Nafshi
Cantor Sally Neff
Cantor Dr. Neil Newman
Cantor Leslie Niren
Cantor Jay O'Brien
Cantor Katie Oringel
Cantor David Lessner Perper
Cantor Juval Porat
Cantor Marshall Portnoy
Rabbi-Cantor Samuel Radwine
Cantor David Reinwald
Cantor Rachel Rhodes
Cantor Janice Roger
Cantor Jennifer Roher
Cantor Elias Roochvarg
Cantor Chanin Rosen
Cantor David Rosen
Cantor Richard Rosenfield
Professor Joyce Rosenzweig
Cantor Jessica Roskin
Cantor Dr. Bruce Ruben
Cantor Faryn Rudnick
Cantor Benjie Ellen Schiller
Cantor Randall Schloss
Cantors Elena and Sergei Schwartz
Cantor Judith Seplowin
Cantor Wendy Shermet
Cantor Michael Shochet
David Shukiar
Cantor Rabbi Gershon Silins
Cantor Sarah Silverberg
Cantor Rollin Simmons
Cantor Rabbi Raina Siroty
Cantor Jill Spasser
Cantor Deborah Staiman
Cantor Debra Stein
Cantor Faith Steinsnyder
Cantor Jennifer Strauss-Klein
Cantor Seth Warner
Cantor Laurie Weinstein
Cantor Steven Weiss
Rabbi Margaret Wenig
Cantor Josee Wolff
Cantor Ross Wolman
Cantor Julie Yugend-Green
Cantor Shanna Zell
Cantor Sarah Zemel
Cantor Sol Zim

CONTENTS

vii Category Index
viii Introduction
x Acknowledgments
xii From the Editorial Committee
xiv About Eliyahu Schleifer
xv The Songs of Eliyahu Schleifer
xxii Audio Track Information

3	**Ein Kamocha**	אין כמוך
7	**Eil Adon**	אל אדון
12	**Eil Malei Rachamim (for Yom HaShoah)**	אל מלא רחמים (לנשמות קדושי השואה)
15	**Elohai, N'shamah Shenatata Bi**	אלוהי, נשמה שנתת בי
19	**Ashreinu**	אשרינו
21	**Bayom Hahu**	ביום ההוא
23	**B'Rosh HaShanah**	בראש השנה
29	**Baruch She-amar**	ברוך שאמר
32	**B'rachah LaCholim (Mi Shebeirach for Healing)**	ברכה לחולים (מי שברך לרפואה)
34	**Hin'ni He-ani Mima-as**	הנני העני ממעש
40	**Hin'ni Ha-aniyah Mima-as (The Female Cantor's Prayer)**	הנני העניה ממעש
51	**V'ha-eir Eineinu**	והאר עינינו
53	**V'ha-arev Na**	והערב נא
55	**V'sham'ru**	ושמרו
58	**Micah, Thus He Said**	כֹּה אמר מיכה
62	**Ki Anu Amecha**	כי אנו עמך
67	**Ki Lekach Tov / Eitz Chayim Hi**	כי לקח טוב / עץ חיים היא
70	**Lo Yarei-u**	לא ירעו
73	**Lamdeini Elohai**	למדני אלוהי
77	**Mah Tovu**	מה טובו
81	**Mah Nomar L'fanecha**	מה נאמר לפניך
84	**Modeh / Modah Ani**	מודה אני
87	**Mi Chamochah**	מי כמוכה
90	**K'dushah**	קדושה
92	**R'tzeih**	רצה
96	**Shehu Noteh Shamayim**	שהוא נוטה שמים
98	**Shehashalom Shelo**	שהשלום שלו

WEEKDAY SERVICE —

77 Mah Tovu מה טובו
84 Modeh / Modah Ani מודה אני
15 Elohai, N'shamah Shenatata Bi אלוהי, נשמה שנתת בי
19 Ashreinu אשרינו
53 V'ha-arev Na והערב נא
51 V'ha-eir Eineinu והאר עינינו
87 Mi Chamochah מי כמוכה
32 B'rachah LaCholim ברכה לחולים
70 Lo Yarei-u לא ירעו
67 Ki Lekach Tov / Eitz Chayim Hi כי לקח טוב / עץ חיים היא
96 Shehu Noteh Shamayim שהוא נוטה שמים
21 Bayom Hahu ביום ההוא
98 Shehashalom Shelo שהשלום שלו

SHABBAT EVENING —

92 R'tzeih רצה
73 Lamdeini Elohai למדני אלוהי
32 B'rachah LaCholim ברכה לחולים
96 Shehu Noteh Shamayim שהוא נוטה שמים
21 Bayom Hahu ביום ההוא
98 Shehashalom Shelo שהשלום שלו

SHABBAT MORNING —

77 Mah Tovu מה טובו
84 Modeh / Modah Ani מודה אני
15 Elohai, N'shamah Shenatata Bi אלוהי, נשמה שנתת בי
53 V'ha-arev Na והערב נא
19 Ashreinu אשרינו
29 Baruch She-amar ברוך שאמר
7 Eil Adon אל אדון
51 V'ha-eir Eineinu והאר עינינו
87 Mi Chamochah מי כמוכה
90 K'dushah קדושה
92 R'tzeih רצה
73 Lamdeini Elohai למדני אלוהי
3 Ein Kamocha אין כמוך
70 Lo Yarei-u לא ירעו
32 B'rachah LaCholim ברכה לחולים
67 Ki Lekach Tov / Eitz Chayim Hi כי לקח טוב / עץ חיים היא
96 Shehu Noteh Shamayim שהוא נוטה שמים
21 Bayom Hahu ביום ההוא
55 V'sham'ru ושמרו
98 Shehashalom Shelo שהשלום שלו

HIGH HOLY DAYS —

34 Hin'ni He-ani Mima-as הנני העני ממעש
40 Hin'ni Ha-aniyah Mima-as הנני העניה ממעש
77 Mah Tovu מה טובו
84 Modeh / Modah Ani מודה אני
15 Elohai, N'shamah Shenatata Bi אלוהי, נשמה שנתת בי
53 V'ha-arev Na והערב נא
19 Ashreinu אשרינו
51 V'ha-eir Eineinu והאר עינינו
23 B'Rosh HaShanah בראש השנה
73 Lamdeini Elohai למדני אלוהי
3 Ein Kamocha אין כמוך
70 Lo Yarei-u לא ירעו
32 B'rachah LaCholim ברכה לחולים
67 Ki Lekach Tov / Eitz Chayim Hi כי לקח טוב / עץ חיים היא
96 Shehu Noteh Shamayim שהוא נוטה שמים
21 Bayom Hahu ביום ההוא
62 Ki Anu Amecha כי אנו עמך
81 Mah Nomar L'fanecha מה נאמר לפניך

SERMON ANTHEMS —

19 Ashreinu אשרינו
62 Ki Anu Amecha כי אנו עמך
73 Lamdeini Elohai למדני אלוהי
70 Lo Yarei-u לא ירעו
81 Mah Nomar L'fanecha מה נאמר לפניך
58 Micah, Thus He Said כֹּה אמר מיכה
98 Shehashalom Shelo שהשלום שלו
53 V'ha-arev Na והערב נא

CONCERT SELECTIONS —

21 Bayom Hahu ביום ההוא
23 B'Rosh HaShanah בראש השנה
7 Eil Adon אל אדון
15 Elohai, N'shamah Shenatata Bi אלוהי, נשמה שנתת בי
40 Hin'ni Ha-aniyah Mima-as הנני העניה ממעש
62 Ki Anu Amecha כי אנו עמך
67 Ki Lekach Tov / Eitz Chayim Hi כי לקח טוב / עץ חיים היא
73 Lamdeini Elohai למדני אלוהי
70 Lo Yarei-u לא ירעו
81 Mah Nomar L'fanecha מה נאמר לפניך
58 Micah, Thus He Said כֹּה אמר מיכה
92 R'tzeih רצה
98 Shehashalom Shelo שהשלום שלו

The name of this anthology, *Mizmor L'Eli*, is intended to express a double meaning: "A Song of Eli" (like "Mizmor L'David" in the Psalms) and "A Song to My God." The anthology contains twenty-seven of my liturgical melodies and cantorial recitatives.

In my youth I indulged in musical composition, and at one time I aspired to become a composer. But I was discouraged by one of the teachers at the Jerusalem Conservatory of Music, a well-known composer (who shall remain nameless) to whom I showed some of my compositions. With a tired voice that showed his disappointment at his own profession, he asked rhetorically, "Why should a young man aspire to become a composer!? It is a useless profession, there is nothing good in it. Better become a musicologist." And this indeed was what I became, in addition to my cantorial career. I should admit that even when I write music now, I do not consider myself a composer, but rather a melodist.

The need to write melodies and cantorial recitatives for the Reform synagogue came in 1980, when I began to act as cantor and teacher at the Hebrew Union College–Jewish Institute of Religion in Jerusalem. At that time there were only rabbinic and archeological students on campus, and I wrote easy congregational melodies, such as the "Ashreinu" in this anthology. In 1986, the School of Sacred Music, HUC-JIR, started the first Year in Israel program for the cantorial students, and a year later, I was appointed as director of the cantorial studies at the Jerusalem campus. I then engaged Cantor Chaim Feifel, *z"l*, to serve as a cantorial coach, and we both wrote melodies and cantorial recitatives for the students. Since both of us came from a traditional background, our idea was to compose music for the Reform liturgy in the traditional style of the Eastern-European *chazanut*.

Our personal styles differed, however; while Chaim was influenced by his teacher, Leib Glantz, and his mystical approach to *chazanut*, mine was influenced by my teacher, Zalman Rivlin, and his emotional yet sober approach that strove for a simple and clean melodic line. Both of us believed that the foundation of *chazanut* should be the traditional *nusach* chants and that the melodies should make use of the traditional cantorial modes. At the same time, we believed that we should abandon the long-winded recitatives that were overloaded with virtuoso passages and were burdened by repetitions of words and phrases. We opted for simpler ones that would better appeal to modern congregations. During his later years, Chaim served as teacher at Tel Aviv Cantorial Institute, and some of his recitatives were published there. He died in the year 2020 and left many melodies and recitatives that still await publication.

My melodies and recitatives also waited for a long time. Meanwhile, some of them were performed by my students in Israel, North America, and Europe. Others were sung by a few congregations without knowing who composed them. This meant that I reached anonymity, the highest level to which a synagogue composer could aspire. I am fortunate that Transcontinental Music Publications, under the directorship of Joe Eglash, undertook to publish them, albeit at the risk that they might lose their anonymity.

Composing music for liturgical texts is a sacred mission for me, while at the same time it is a means for entertaining my soul. I always start with the text, never with a melody. Most of the prayers I know by heart, and yet I study them again and again until a melody germinates in my mind. Thus, most of my melodies could be considered as "logogenic" (a tune inspired by the flow of text), to use Alfred Einstein's term from his 1954 essay "Words and Music." When this happens, I work on the melody like a potter on clay to try to shape it properly.

Sometimes this happens instantaneously, but most of the time it needs some toil and struggle to bring the melody to the best form I can and to make sure that the melody agrees with the text. Thus, I try to preserve the right accentuation by placing the stressed syllables on accentuated notes and giving them a higher note then the unstressed ones (which is not always possible when text and melody need to compromise). I pay special attention to the rhythm of the text (for instance, I try to present *sh'va na* syllables with relatively short notes and the accented syllables with longer notes).

I am a staunch believer in the traditional *nusach,* and while we are witnessing a decline in the knowledge and use of *nusach* in all the Ashkenazic denominations, I believe that the traditional *nusach* will come back (perhaps in a different format or guise), and it will enjoy a resurrection. I also believe that behind my melodies there is always a notion of *nusach* even when they deviate from it.

My cantorial recitatives spring out of a longtime experience in improvisation. During my youth, I was raised on the necessity to extemporize on prayer texts, especially on the long ones, and I was fortunate to listen to some great cantors improvise during the services. I believe that this manner of liturgical singing, which is unfortunately rarely used by cantors today, could be compared to what a French chef does when preparing a meal in front of clients. It is much fun for the cantor and a delight for congregants who are willing to open their ears for such melodic streams. In my experience, even listeners who are not familiar with this kind of creation may feel the spirit of the improvised piece when it is well done. Moreover, while I enjoy the fun of an unfolding melody or recitative as they come out of my mouth, the process fills me with a sacred sense, as if I would prepare a melodic sacrifice for God. During the improvisation I pay particular attention to seminal words of the prayer, and I try to express them in melody; thus I hope that the recitative becomes a kind of a "mini sermon" on the prayer.

Many years of experience have made me aware that the repetitions of a prayer, week in and week out, tend to freeze the improvisation. The danger of such freezing is that the recitative may become a routine piece. The sign that a repeated improvisation has been covered with the patina of routine is when the congregation sings the frozen improvisation with the cantor. The good side of it nevertheless is that the frozen notes could be worked out as an artistic piece. Such, I believe, were the origins of many cantorial pieces of the so-called Golden Age of Chazanut, and this is what I strove to create in my written cantorial recitatives. For better or for worse, my written recitatives, such as the "Hin'ni" prayers in this book, are the fruits of such frozen improvisations.

In addition to the influence of Eastern European *chazanut* on my recitatives, the melodies in this volume are influenced by Chasidic *nigunim*, by Israeli folk tunes, and sometimes even by Romanian pastoral or Gypsy melodic patterns. Thus, they represent me, an Israeli sabra whose father's family came from Lemberg (now Lviv in the Ukraine) and settled in Jerusalem in 1842 and whose mother immigrated in 1935 from Transylvania (in Romania).

I hope that this anthology will be useful for our cantors and the music will find favor with God and humans.

Cantor Eliyahu Schleifer, PhD
March 2024 / Adar II 5784

› My first thanks go to my parents, *z"l*: To my father, Ze-ev Velvl Schleifer, who always reminded me of the Levite origins of our family and was proud that I followed in the footsteps of the Biblical musicians. To my mother, Peninah-Perl Schleifer (ne. Fried), who made enormous efforts to support my musical education, even during hard economic times. Thanks to my sisters, Adina Marx *z"l*, Naomi Schleifer-Ackerman, and Dr. Yehudit Avnir, for their spiritual support and for tolerating the long and tedious hours of my practicing the violin, French horn, and voice.

› I owe many thanks to my rebbe and *chazanut* teacher Cantor Shlomo Zalman Rivlin, of blessed memory. My cantorial style is much influenced by his singing and teaching, and if you detect a motif or more that resembles his music, it is not there by mere coincidence.

› To the deans of HUC–JIR, Jerusalem, for supporting my musical activities. I remember with special affection Dr. Michael L. Klein, *z"l*, whose love for *chazanut* matched his enormous knowledge of Judaica, and who would preface every conversation on mundane things with a long discourse over classical cantorial pieces. I also owe thanks to the interim dean, Rabbi Uri Regev, who gave me the folk melody for "B'Rosh HaShanah," to the deans Rabbi Dr. Michael Marmur, whose scholarship, sharp wit, and musicality inspired me, and to the latest dean, Rabbi Dr. Naamah Kelman-Ezrachi. I want to thank my dear friend and colleague Rabbi Paul (Shaul) R. Feinberg. For over two decades we shared the pulpit at the Murstein Synagogue of HUC–JIR, Jerusalem, and he encouraged my musical activities for the synagogue.

› To the past directors of the School of Sacred Music: Rabbi-Cantor Jon Haddon, Rabbi Dr. Lawrence Hoffman, Cantor Richard Cohn, Cantor Dr. Bruce Ruben, and the present director, Cantor Jill Abramson. I remember with special love Cantor Israel (Izzy) Goldstein, *z"l*, for his cooperation with me for over twenty years. Izzy will be remembered for his special mastery of traditional *chazanut*. He deeply inspired me with his outstanding cantorial improvisation and his mastery of the cantorial modes.

› To my cantorial partners at the pulpit of the Murstein Synagogue of HUC–JIR, Jerusalem: Cantor Dr. Daniel Ziff, *z"l*, Cantor Alane Katzew, and Cantor Mikhal Shiff-Matter, and the past and present coordinators of cantorial studies, Cantor Tamar Havilio and Cantor Sarah Grabiner.

› To the pianists at HUC–JIR, Jerusalem: Dan Bleicher, Olga Borisovsky, and Gregory Shifrin, and especially Monica Gorlen Fallon and the present pianist Anastasia Sobolev.

› To the cantors who contributed to the recordings that accompany this anthology: Jill Abramson, David Berger, Joshua Breitzer, Evan Cohen, Galit Dadoun Cohen, and Sarah Grabiner. Thank you to pianists Aya Laipsker-Schleifer, Joyce Rosenzweig, and Anastasia Sobolev.

› To those without whose initiative, efforts, and work this anthology would not become a reality:
–First and foremost, Cantor Evan Cohen of Kehilat Har-El in Jerusalem, who was the first editor of the music and accompanied the anthology throughout the process of its publication.
–Cantor Claire Franco, past president of the American Conference of Cantors (ACC), who many years ago raised the initial funds for creating the anthology and has supported it ever since.

–Cantor Ross Wolman, who after our meeting in Jerusalem about two years ago initiated the final publication, and Cantor David Berger, who encouraged it.

› Special thanks to the arrangers of the works in this volume: Raymond Goldstein, Anastasia Sobolev, Doron Schleifer, and Joyce Rosenzweig. They enhanced my simple melodies by adding depth and beauty, and thus they raised their musical level to real compositions.

› To all my former students and other cantors who have contributed funds to make this publication possible: *May your voices rise, and your singing be meaningful and successful.*

› Above all, I would like to thank Mr. Joe Eglash, director and editor in chief of Transcontinental Music Publications, for taking the anthology under his wings, for his high standards of publishing, and for his meticulous work on the form and contents of the volume.

Finally, I would like to express my endless love to my wife, pianist Aya Laipsker Schleifer, partner of my life and my music for over fifty years, and to our two musicians, our sons Doron and Uri Schleifer, with whom we share our love and our music.

Cantor Eliyahu Schleifer, PhD
March 2024 / Adar II 5784

With great joy and excitement, we are truly blessed to share with you *Mizmor L'Eli: Eliyahu Schleifer Anthology*. Although the initial work for the project began in 2008, after many years this anthology has finally come to fruition in 2024, with the publication of twenty-seven liturgical melodies and cantorial recitatives of Cantor Eliyahu Schleifer, PhD.

Eli, as he is fondly known, was appointed as director of cantorial studies at the Jerusalem campus of HUC–JIR in 1986. Today, in his "semi-retirement," he continues to teach students at HUC, serves as an instructor in the cantorial program of Geiger College in Germany, and pursues his own Jewish musicological research. Eli has had a profound influence on generations of cantors from around the world; for many, he was their first teacher of *chazanut*, opening their eyes and ears to the beauty, majesty, and intellectual and emotional depth of our musical heritage. Legendary for his encyclopedic knowledge of anything concerning Jewish music, liturgy, and the Hebrew language, together with his openness to answer (in phenomenal detail) any question posed to him, Eli has continued to serve as an invaluable resource for his students, his past students and now colleagues, and the Jewish musical world.

There are precious few people in the Jewish music world who have earned the universal respect of cantors, music directors, rabbis, educators, and academics from across the denominational spectrum. Eliyahu Schleifer has gained this respect and, even more, is truly loved by his students. Seen as the ultimate authority whose answers are definitive in virtually all areas of Jewish musical knowledge, Eli has a unique talent of inspiring people to want to learn more. Most importantly, this vast and unmatched mastery of his field is paired with a gentleness, humility, and unassuming nature that stands at the center of Eli's personality and is felt throughout his compositions. In a Schleifer piece, adherence to traditional *nusach* and uncompromising textual precision finds expression in a blend of congregational melody and cantorial beauty. We hope you will feel this spirit throughout the pieces in this anthology.

When considering which of Eli's pieces would be included in this anthology, the editorial committee's goal was to focus on compositions and recitatives suitable for today's Reform synagogue that truly reflect Eli's approach to *t'filah*, elucidated in Eli's preface to the anthology. While some of the compositions are well-known, the majority are published here for the very first time. We strove to provide a balance of compositions with beautiful arrangements for piano by Joyce Rosenzweig, Anastasia Sobolev, Doron Schleifer, and Raymond Goldstein, lead sheets with chords, and *a cappella* chants. While many of the pieces were composed for worship at the Murstein Synagogue at the Jerusalem campus of HUC, at which services that Eli led were accompanied by piano, all of the compositions can also be sung without instrumental accompaniment if desired.

Another factor taken into consideration by the committee was to choose compositions that fulfilled a specific need. Sometimes this was dictated by the needs of today's egalitarian synagogue, and hence a new setting was created of "Hin'ni" for female cantors ("Hin'ni Haaniyah Mimaas"), both textually and musically. Others were written as requests to Eli by cantors to provide congregational melodies for prayers that would both preserve correct Hebrew accentuation and be true to the *nusach*, such as "Modeh/Modah Ani," "B'rachah LaCholim (Mi Shebeirach for Healing)," or "Baruch She-amar." And others arised from a need by Eli himself, in response to (or even protest against) contemporary practice, to write new settings for our worship that better reflect Eli's aspirations for us as cantors, such as "Ein Kamocha," "V'ha-eir Eineinu," and "Shehu Noteh Shamayim."

Ever the commensurate teacher, we invite you also to pay particular attention to Eli's detailed notes for each of the pieces in the anthology. It will enhance your appreciation and interpretation of each of the compositions, as well as another opportunity to learn from one of the masters of the cantorial arts.

As we sing during the *Hallel*:
Eli atah v'odeka—אלי אתה ואודך, "You are my God, and I will thank You," which in this context can be translated as "You are Eli, and I will thank you!"

The editorial committee of *Mizmor L'Eli*:
Cantor David Berger (KAM Isaiah Israel Congregation, Chicago, Illinois)
Cantor Evan Cohen (Kehilat Har-El, Jerusalem, Israel)
Joel Eglash (director of Transcontinental Music Publications)
Cantor Ross Wolman (Temple Chai, Phoenix, Arizona)

March 2024 / Adar II 5784

ELIYAHU ARIE SCHLEIFER (ELI) was born in Jerusalem in 1939. At the age of three and a half, he began his education at the *cheder* and the yeshivah Etz Chaim. At the age of ten, he moved to the Tachkemony grade school and then continued at the high school of the Hebrew University.

He began his musical training at the age of five as a *meshorer* (choirboy) and later as junior cantor at the Shirat Yisrael Institute, where he studied *chazanut* with the master of cantorial art Cantor Shlomo-Zalman Rivlin. At the age of ten he began studying the violin at the Jerusalem New Conservatory of Music, and later he also took up the French horn.

During the years 1958–1960, he fulfilled his army duties as musician in the IDF band and symphonic orchestra, and after his discharge, he continued French-horn studies at the Rubin Academy of Music, Jerusalem, graduating in 1964. Concurrently, he studied Jewish philosophy and Kabbalah at Hebrew University.

During the years 1964–1967, he served as assistant to the ethnomusicologist Dr. Edith Gerson-Kiwi, researching the music of the Jewish communities of Israel. He also played the French horn at Kol Yisrael (now Jerusalem) Symphony and appeared occasionally as an additional French-horn and Wagner-tuba player with the Israel Philharmonic Orchestra.

In 1968, he began academic studies in music history and theory at the University of Chicago, where he received the MA and PhD degrees in musicology. During his sojourn in Chicago, he served as cantor at the Conservative synagogue South Side Hebrew Congregation. Returning to Israel in 1976, he taught music history at the Rubin Academy of Music, Jerusalem, and served as senior lecturer in the department of musicology at Tel Aviv University. In his public capacity as musicologist, he was appointed several times as judge on the committee of the Israel Prime Minister's Prize for Musical Composition, and for a few years, he was chairman of the Israeli Musicological Society.

In 1980, he began his work at Hebrew Union College–Jewish Institute of Religion, Jerusalem, as cantor and teacher, sharing the pulpit with Rabbi Paul (Shaul) R. Feinberg, and in 1987, he was appointed associate professor of sacred music and director of cantorial studies. During his years as teacher at HUC–JIR, he composed liturgical melodies for the students and was active in researching Ashkenazic synagogue music and its history. Upon his retirement, in 2010, he was granted the honorary degree of doctor of humane letters (DHL) by HUC–JIR. Then, for a few years, he served as director of the cantorial school at the Abraham Geiger College and Potsdam University in Berlin, Germany.

On August 10, 2022, the Eighteenth World Congress of Jewish Studies honored him with a concert of his liturgical music at Hebrew University, Mount Scopus. A similar concert was given three months later by the Abraham Geiger College in Berlin. He now continues his research on Ashkenazic synagogue music at the Israel National Library and the Jewish Music Research Center of the Hebrew University.

Prof. Eliyahu Schleifer is married to Aya Schleifer (pianist), and they enjoy their two sons, Doron (countertenor singer) and Uri (violinist).

Ein Kamocha אין כמוך

"Ein Kamocha" for the Torah service was written to replace Salomon Sulzer's "Ein Kamocha" and Abraham Dunajewski's "Av Harachamim." Originally these were wonderful compositions, and they are still beautiful when they are well performed. Unfortunately, however, they are sung today in distorted versions. Every time I hear them at services, I am filled with compassion for these two wonderful composers, as they spin in their graves. Therefore, I decided to propose a new piece for the Torah service to release the two masters from this doom. My "Ein Kamocha–Av Harachamim" is written in a mixture of a declamatory style for the cantor's recitatives and patterns of Israeli folk songs for the congregational melodies. I have inserted a hint to "Hatikvah" for the words that mention Zion.

Eil Adon אל אדון

This beautiful anthem, praising God for creating the sun, moon, and stars, is part of the "Yotzeir" (praising the Creator) benediction on Shabbat morning. Among the Chasidim, it is customary to sing it either as a waltz or a march. Many prefer the march, since it is associated with royalty and thus it may represent God's majesty and power. My setting is inspired by this Chasidic genre, which in turn is influenced by the style of Polish military marches. Like the latter, it is written in the major mode with a "Minore" section inserted in the middle. The melody ends with a triumphant return to the major mode. The text is the original Ashkenazic version, which I prefer to the modified Sephardic one that is printed in some Reform prayer books.

Eil Malei Rachamim (for Yom HaShoah) אל מלא רחמים (לנשמות קדושי השואה)

The text is my shortened version of the memorial prayer for the martyrs of the Shoah. Unlike the current versions of the prayer, this one does not mention names of concentration and death camps. I believe that mentioning just a few of them might diminish the memory of the numerous other ones and would neglect the Jews who were murdered in different other ways. The text includes a symbolic call for the earth not to cover up the martyrs' blood and that their cry would never be diminished (following the words of Job 16:18). It ends with a plea for their everlasting repose and the hope for universal peace. The cantorial recitative begins with the traditional Ahavah Rabbah mode on C, and it climbs to F and B-flat minor as the emotion of the prayer intensifies. Toward the end, when the prayer mentions God's mercy and the hope for peace, the recitative returns to F-minor. As is customary in some emotional cantorial pieces, the piece ends a fourth above its beginning, with the Ahavah Rabbah mode on F.

Elohai, N'shamah Shenatata Bi אלוהי, נשמה שנתת בי

This is a setting of the Israeli Reform text of the beautiful morning prayer for the human soul. According to the old Jewish lore, our soul departs from our bodies at the night's sleep and returns to us when we wake up. The Israeli Reform version of the prayer expresses the belief that at our death, the soul will be taken by God to eternal life. The Reform version rejects the Orthodox *chatimah* (ending), praising God for returning the soul to dead carcasses. It replaces it with a nobler ending praising God, "in whose hand is the soul of every living creature and the spirit of all human flesh" (a quotation of Job 12:10). The music was written at the request of the then-cantorial student Sarah Pscheidt for our Monday morning services. It was an attempt to counteract the tendency prevalent in our synagogues to chant the first six words of the prayer as a repetitive mantra and neglect the rest of the prayer. The cantorial recitative begins with the invocation, "Elohai" (My God!) as a trumpet call with a long fermata. This also saves the singer from the erroneous combination of "Elohai n'shamah." The music then emphasizes the four occurrences of "atah" (You, O God) in a musical pattern that is varied according to the meaning of the text. The words "Modeh/Modah ani l'fanecha..." (I thank You, Adonai, my God and God of my forefathers and foremothers) are set to a rhythmical melody that should invite the congregation to join in the singing. The same goes for the concluding words "Asher b'yado..." (in whose hand...). The music is in the minor mode (the mode of this section during the weekday morning service) with some digressions to the Dorian mode (minor with a raised sixth) in the Israeli style.

Ashreinu אשרינו

The joyful melody, in the style of Chasidic *nigunei simchah* (melodies of rejoicing) is intended to express our delight in being a link in the chain of Jewish heritage. Joyce Rosenzweig's accompaniment enhances this feeling. The melody was written to begin the Monday morning services at HUC–JIR synagogue on an uplifting tone. It is in the minor mode in which the weekday morning prayers begin.

Bayom Hahu ביום ההוא

The setting of the last words of the prayer "Aleinu L'shabei-ach" is a revised version of a duet for Cantor Lori Corrsin and me. The second part on "Adonai echad ushmo echad" (Adonai will be one, and God's name will be one) begins as a "stretto" imitation between the soprano and bass. The words are then repeated, the bass line supporting the soprano melody. This is meant as a symbol of the unification of God and God's name at the end of days, according to the prophesy of Zechariah (14:9).

B'Rosh HaShanah בראש השנה

The horrifying text from the *Musaf* service of the High Holy Days is the fifth and penultimate part of the poem "Untaneh Tokef," the Jewish "Dies Irrae." It expounds the ancient belief that on Rosh HaShanah human beings are sentenced for life or death and the verdict is sealed on Yom Kippur. The main part of the prayer is a litany of contrasting pairs of calamities such as "who [shall perish] by fire and who by water." Yet despite the harsh words, the Eastern European cantors sang the opening statement, "On Rosh HaShanah they [all human beings] are inscribed and on Yom Kippur [their fates] are sealed," as a congregational refrain on an easy folk-like tune. I based the refrain on a folk tune that I had heard from Rabbi Uri Regev, who served as the dean of HUC–JIR, Jerusalem. As contrast to the easy tune, I built the cantorial recitative as a set of melodic word paintings that are meant to represent the enumerated human calamities. The recitative is highly influenced by the chants of my teacher Cantor Zalman Rivlin, *z"l*. Toward the end, at the words "Mi yanuach umi yanua," the music quotes the traditional *nusach* chant and ends with shofar-like calls to confirm triumphantly that "through return to the right path, through prayer and *tzedakah*, we can transcend the harshness of the decree."

Baruch She-amar ברוך שאמר

The prayer opens the public part of the *Shacharit* morning service and is a set of praises to God the Creator. It extols God as the "One who spoke and the world came to be." It then continues with praises for God's deeds. The prayer ends with the words "Blessed are You, Adonai, Sovereign who is glorified through praise," and it sets the framework for the recitation of the "P'sukei D'zimrah" (psalm verses of praise), which constitute the first section of the *Shacharit* morning service. In most prayer books, the praises are set in a simple litany of phrases, beginning each with the word "Baruch." But the editor of the Israeli Reform siddur *HaAvodah SheBaLev*, Rabbi Yehoram Mazor, preferred to restore an old version in which a set of responses "Baruch hu" and "Baruch sh'mo" ("blessed is the One" and "blessed is God's name") alternate after the verses of praise, thus letting the congregation react to the praises in a set of refrains. Israeli Reform congregations sing this textual version to a simple chant without distinguishing between the cantor's statements and the congregational responses. In addition, the chant is in the minor mode, which is the appropriate one for the *nusach* of this part of the service on weekdays, but not on Shabbat, where it is to be sung in major. Cantor Evan Cohen of Kehilat Har-El in Jerusalem asked me to compose a new piece that would be sung responsively and in the correct *nusach*. I chose to utilize Evan's wonderful vocal ability in order to develop an elaborate melody for the cantor. While the congregational responses remain simple and constant, the cantor's part develops into a set of variations that soar up to a climax, in which some word paintings are incorporated. I have dedicated the new setting to Cantor Evan Cohen, and I am glad that it has become a constant part of the Shabbat morning services at Kehilat Har-El.

B'rachah LaCholim (Mi Shebeirach for Healing) ברכה לחולים (מי שברך לרפואה)

The Ashkenazic cantorial tradition insists that the "Mi Shebeirach" blessing for those in need of healing be chanted in the major mode. The traditional *nusach* formulae for this prayer were based on the fanfare chant of calling up a person for an *aliyah laTorah*. The traditional "Mi Shebeirach" prayer was not considered a supplication, imploring God for the recovery (halachically such pleading was not permitted on Shabbat); it was rather an expression of assurance that God will certainly bless the sick and restore them to good health. Lately, beautiful melodies in the minor mode were composed by able cantors of the Reform Movement. To me, however, they seem sad, and thus they contradict the optimistic tone of the traditional chants. I mentioned my concern to Rabbi Ada Zavidov and Cantor Evan Cohen, and they challenged me to create a new melody in the major mode for Kehilat Har-El, Jerusalem, which I did. This piece is dedicated to Rabbi Zavidov and Cantor Cohen. The melody is modular and consists of three parts: (A) the beginning of the traditional "Mi Shebeirach" prayer; (B) a tune to be hummed in a lower volume during the name reading; and (C) Moses's prayer for the healing of his sister Miriam, "Eil na r'fa na lah" (Numbers 12:13), is set to melodic sequences in the feminine, masculine, and plural forms. The order of the parts may change according to custom of the synagogue (see the note at the end of the music).

Hin'ni He-ani Mima-as (for male cantors) הנני העני ממעש

"Hin'ni" is the cantor's prayer for the success of his mission as the emissary of the congregation before God, and it has been one of the highlights of the cantorial recitatives during the High Holy Days. In the Orthodox ritual, it is sung before the *Musaf* service; in some Reform congregations, before the selections from the same service or before the beginning of the *Maariv* service on the eve of Rosh HaShanah. Some Conservative and Reform congregations rejected it altogether, fearing that the cantor might abuse it by merely showing off his or her voice. According to an ancient tradition, the cantor began singing it from the pews of the poor people at the back of the synagogue, to emphasize the words "Poor in worthy deeds I am." He then continued singing it as he walked to the cantor's pulpit. The text in this setting and the English translation are based on Philip Birnbaum's *High Holyday Prayer Book* (New York: Hebrew Publishing Company, 1951). This version is intended for male cantors. Female cantors may prefer the ensuing feminine version, "Hin'ni Haaniyah Mimaas." This cantorial recitative is based on traditional *nusach* patterns, and it aspires to present the drama of the words in musical notes. As I wrote it, I set before my eyes the image of my teacher Cantor Zalman Rivlin and the way in which he would express the prayer emotionally and musically. I also tried to follow the path of the old cantorial improvisations. As was customary in such improvisations, and as is still common in jazz improvisation, the music digresses at times quoting fragments of traditional or folk melodies to emphasize certain words or seminal phrases. If needed, the cantor may shorten the prayer by skipping the "whispering" part at the end of the prayer (pickup to measure 73 to measure 93) or whisper it without the melody.

Hin'ni Ha-aniyah Mima-as (The Female Cantor's Prayer) הנני העניה ממעש

For a long time, I toyed with the idea of writing a female version for the cantor's prayer "Hin'ni He-ani Mimaas," but only recently did I arrive at what I believe is a successful female cantorial recitative. For this I had to modify the text, not only by automatically changing the masculine to the feminine gender, but also by eliminating certain phrases and adding other more suitable ones. For example, the original text describes the ideal *chazan* as having a long beard, which of course is ridiculous for a female prayer. I was inspired by the text of the female version in the new Conservative *machzor Lev Shalem*. But I felt that additional changes were needed to represent the musical and liturgical aspirations of the female cantor. I therefore rewrote some of it and inserted the request that God accept the cantor's prayer just as God cherished the prayer of Hannah and the songs of Miriam and Deborah. The musical recitative is based on my male version of "Hin'ni," but the music was rewritten taking in consideration the nature and characteristics of the female voice. The piano part added by Doron Schleifer is intended to support the cantor in this long prayer.

V'ha-eir Eineinu והאר עינינו

The text is the second section of the prayer "Ahavah Rabbah Ahavtanu," which leads to the recitation of the "Sh'ma" in the morning *Shacharit* prayer. The old custom was to chant the entire prayer in the Ahavah Rabbah mode. But over fifty years ago, cantors began to alter the end of the prayer and sing it in the major mode, with the intention to lead the congregation into the "Sulzerian" melody of "Sh'ma." This change was then followed by another one, where cantors began to sing melodies in minor before modulating into the major mode—the most famous of these being Carlebach's "V'ha-eir Eineinu." The latter melody, however, was composed not for this prayer, but for non-liturgical joyful occasions. It is a wonderful melody for ceremonies like the *hakafot* on Simchat Torah, but in my opinion it does not belong in the "Ahavah Rabbah" prayer. I therefore composed another melody that, I believe, fits the text better. It begins in minor and ends in major leading smoothly to "Sh'ma," and it contains elements of Chasidic melodies, especially in the section that asks God to restore us as a nation in our land.

V'ha-arev Na והערב נא

The prayer called "Birkat HaTorah" is the benediction recited before the public study of portions from the Mishnah. Traditionally it is also said at the beginning of the daily morning prayers, and it is usually followed by a portion from the Mishnah. We bless God for the commandment to study Torah, and we ask God that that the study be sweet to us and that we and our future generations continue studying forever. The chant was composed for the Monday morning services at HUC–JIR, Jerusalem. It is based on a variant of the study mode (*lern-steiger*) in minor, which is used for studying the Mishnah.

V'sham'ru ושמרו

The biblical verses (Exodus 31:16–17) that enjoin us to keep Shabbat as a covenant between God and us are recited two times during the Shabbat services (evening and morning) and once more before the *Kiddush* after the Shabbat morning service. The text is a stern commandment, yet, at the *Kiddush* it is customary to sing it to a joyful melody. Thus, we express our delight in the *Oneg Shabbat* (the delight of Shabbat) as we are to partake in the wine and bread of the *Kiddush*. The melody, in the Chasidic style of *nigunei simchah*, is intended specifically for the *Kiddush* and not for the same text during the Shabbat services.

Micah, Thus He Said כֹּה אמר מיכה

The Reform Movement was always inspired by the prophet Micah's insistence to center the essence of Judaism on three principles: "To do justly and love mercy and walk humbly with your God." Moved by Micah's vision, I tried to give it my own musical expression. The text is my English paraphrase of the Book of Micah, 6:6–8. The music envisions a *magid*, an itinerant preacher, who wanders from one shtetl to another and delivers his sermon on the prophet Micah in a musical style that is typical of the chants of the *magidim*. It begins with a dramatic recitative in which the perplexed Micah asks God whether one should worship God by sacrificing many animals, even by sacrificing one's own son. And it ends with God's simple answer reducing the human obligations to God to the three moral principles. This is musically expressed by a simple melody in triple time.

Ki Anu Amecha כי אנו עמך

This is one of the most beloved penitential prayers on Yom Kippur, since it expresses the bond between God and us in endearing terms. We are God's children, God's flock, and God is our parent and our shepherd; we are God's beloved, and God is our lover. This setting, in Hebrew and English, is based on the text of the machzor *Gates of Repentance*. The piece begins with a quotation of a traditional melody for "S'lach Lanu" (Forgive Us), it continues with a setting of the Hebrew words to a slow waltz melody, then follows the English translation in a free "parlando" recitative, and finally the Hebrew waltz returns. I wrote this piece for then-cantorial student Marcy Kadin, and it was tailored to her deep alto voice. Therefore, originally the music was in a much lower key. I instructed Marcy to sing it as if she were "waltzing with God." Marcy sang it for the first time on the eve of Yom Kippur, and to our astonishment, when the Hebrew words returned, the entire congregation sang them with her, without ever hearing it before. The piece became a favorite in the HUC–JIR Yom Kippur services, and later Cantor Tamar Havilio, who served as coordinator of cantorial studies at HUC–JIR, Jerusalem, recorded it as the theme song of her album that carried the same name.

Ki Lekach Tov / Eitz Chayim Hi כי לקח טוב / עץ חיים היא

The biblical text (Proverbs 4:2, 3:18, 3:17; Lamentations 5:21) is sung at the end of the Torah service, when the Torah scroll is returned to the holy ark. Thus, it functions as a departure song for the Torah, with the hope to return to it next week. The melody was written at the request of pianist Joyce Rosenzweig, for a Shabbat afternoon (*Minchah*) service during an HUC–JIR faculty retreat. Therefore, the last verse is intoned by the cantor in the *nusach* melody of the Shabbat *Minchah* service, and it anticipates the traditional chant for the following *Kaddish*. The music begins with a short cantorial recitative on "Ki lekach tov…" and precedes with a triple-meter melody inspired by Israeli song composers such as Sasha Argov. The melodic line is meant to depict a growing tree. The music is suitable for bar/bat mitzvah celebrations during the Shabbat *Minchah* services, but it has been sung during the morning services as well. The piece is dedicated to Joyce Rosenzweig.

Lo Yarei-u לא ירעו

Among other options for opening the Torah service, the Reform prayer books suggest the biblical verses Isaiah 11:9 and Micah 4:4, as they represent the hope for the ideal human conditions during the messianic era. The music was written for the services at HUC–JIR, Jerusalem, in a combination of a Chasidic-style refrain in minor and verses in the style of Israeli songs in the Dorian mode.

Lamdeini Elohai למדני אלוהי

Leah Goldberg's wonderful poem asks God for the gift of prayer and praise, for the ability to enjoy nature and to avoid a meaningless routine life. It echoes the aspirations of men and women of our time and has therefore become an inspiring prayer in the liturgy of the Reform Movement. I composed the melody with special attention to the words and their emotional impact, and I intended to shape it as an Israeli folk song. The two stanzas are first sung by the cantor, then by the congregation; the cantor then concludes with the beginning segments of both stanzas as a summary of the poem.

Mah Tovu מה טובו

The melody of "Mah Tovu" was written to open the Shabbat morning services at HUC–JIR, Jerusalem. We used to start with a 6/8 meter Chasidic *nigun* in the minor mode, and this setting was intended to serve as a sequel to it. Soon after composing the piece, I tried it during a Shabbat morning service, and I decided that it needed corrections. But our associate cantor, Mikhal Shiff-Matter, and our pianist, Monica Fallon, snatched the music from my hands, and they did not allow any changes. And so, in this imperfect form it is sung to this day. The melody is set as two cantorial verses with a congregational refrain. The melody is in a mixture of the Aeolian (natural minor) and Dorian (minor with a raised sixth) modes, as is common in Israeli songs.

Mah Nomar L'fanecha מה נאמר לפניך

"What can we tell You, O Dweller on High?" The words from the Yom Kippur confessional prayer suggest that we cannot hide our wrongdoings from the omniscient God, who probes the depths of the human soul. The music attempts to capture the meaning of the words using musical imagery for the sentence "You penetrate the compartments of the belly and examine the kidneys and the heart," as these represent the ancient biblical concept that the belly is the seat of the intellect, the kidneys are the domain of our moral consciousness, and the heart is the source of thought. The music was written for my son Doron, who as a child sang this solo at the HUC–JIR synagogue. Many years later, he reciprocated by arranging the piece for voice and piano.

Modeh / Modah Ani מודה אני

Originally, this prayer was created to be said immediately upon waking up in the morning, while one was still in bed and even before washing one's hands. Therefore, it does not mention God's name. In the Reform Movement, however, it was incorporated into the public morning service, and it became the first prayer of *Shacharit*. As a member of Kehilat Har-El in Jerusalem, I was annoyed to hear this endeared prayer sung every Shabbat morning to a trite ditty with the wrong Hebrew accentuation. I pointed this out to Cantor Evan Cohen, and he challenged me to write a new melody with the correct accentuation, which I did. Ever since then this melody replaced the old one, for which change I am grateful to Cantor Cohen. The light melody is intended as an easy opener for the yet un-warmed congregation. It is usually sung *a cappella*, but Anastasia Sobolev's accompaniment is a welcome addition, as it consists of harp-like chord patterns that may suggest awakening from sleep.

Mi Chamochah מי כמוכה

Cantorial tradition mandates that on Shabbat morning, the prayers between the "Sh'ma" and the *Amidah*, including "Mi Chamochah," be sung in the Ahavah Rabbah mode. This mode is emotionally versatile—it can sound sad or joyful. Obviously, "Mi Chamochah," which is part of Moses's and Miriam's "Song at the Sea," should explore the joyful end of the emotional spectrum. I therefore composed the music in a klezmer style, with melodic leaps that are meant to express exuberance and vigor. As is common in this mode, the melody is in ABA form, where section A is in D Ahavah Rabbah, section B modulates to Adonai Malach on G, then the music returns to the AR mode.

K'dushah קדושה

The "K'dushah," the most sacred part of the *Amidah* prayer, was traditionally sung on Shabbat morning in the Ahavah Rabbah mode. During the nineteenth century, under the German influence, the Reform Movement preferred to sing it in the major mode. Later, music was composed to it in the minor mode, and an especially popular version in the Reform Movement is still Bonia Shur's, composed as a folk-like melody in natural minor. The present setting is an attempt to restore the "K'dushah" of the Shabbat *Shacharit Amidah* to the traditional Ahavah Rabbah mode. The basic mode of the piece is D AR, but as has been traditional to this mode, the music modulates to the minor mode or the Adonai Malach mode on the fourth degree (G). The congregational responses are simple tunes in the original key, and as is also common in such settings, the words "V'hu yashmi-einu…" are sung to a Chasidic-like tune.

R'tzeih רצה

The fifth of the seven benedictions of the Shabbat *Amidah* is a plea for the restoration of the Divine Presence to Zion, and I consider it the most emotional of these benedictions. I tried to represent my feelings in the music. The text is one of the versions in *Gates of Prayer*, which includes the phrase asking God to pour the divine spirit upon us. According to the cantorial tradition, the music is in the Ahavah Rabbah mode on D, with the traditional digression to the minor mode on the fourth degree (G). Also, according to tradition, the words "V'techezenah eineinu…" (Let our eyes behold Your loving return to Zion) are sung to a folk-like rhythmic melody. The music is the first solo that I composed for my son Doron, when he was about eight years old.

Shehu Noteh Shamayim שהוא נוטה שמים

For many years I was suffering from the so-called traditional melody for "Shehu Noteh Shamayim" of the "Aleinu L'shabei-ach" prayer. The "Itsy Bitsy Spider" nursery ditty, I believed, was not the proper musical expression for the lofty idea of the prayer. Several times I attempted to write a melody that would do justice to the words that talked about God who spread out the heavens and established the earth, whose throne and *Shechinah* are in the heavens above, but I was not satisfied with the results. One day, while teaching at the Abraham Geiger College in Berlin, I was traveling on a train that signaled every stop with the motif a-d'-d'-e'-f#'-e'-d'-b"-a" from a German folk tune. "Aha," I said to myself, "strangely enough, this could be the proper beginning for such melody." Then the melody came quickly to me; I taught it to my cantorial students, and it caught on immediately. The melody is not easy to sing, as it spans an octave and a half, and yet it has become "the" melody for "Shehu Noteh Shamayim" in various Liberal and Conservative synagogues in Germany.

Shehashalom Shelo שהשלום שלו

The prayer for this piece is a verse in the Shabbat table song "Baruch Adonai Yom Yom" by Shimon ben Yitzchak, one of the greatest songwriters (*pay'tanim*) of medieval Germany. It is usually sung during the afternoon meals of Shabbat, mainly by the Chasidim. I wrote the melody at the request of then-cantorial student Lauren Bandman, who needed a song on peace for the end of a Shabbat service. The melody is in the style of Chasidic *z'mirot*, especially the middle section, which can be sung as a duet in parallel thirds.

Track	Title	Singer	Pianist
1	**Ein Kamocha** **	Cantor Joshua Breitzer	Joyce Rosenzweig
2	**Eil Adon** ****	Cantor Eliyahu Schleifer	Aya Laipsker-Schleifer
3	**Eil Malei Rachamim (for Yom HaShoah)** **	Cantor Joshua Breitzer	
4	**Elohai, N'shamah Shenatata Bi** ****	Cantor Eliyahu Schleifer	Aya Laipsker-Schleifer
5	**Ashreinu** *	Cantor Eliyahu Schleifer and group	Aya Laipsker-Schleifer
6	**Bayom Hahu** *	Cantor Sarah Grabiner and Cantor Eliyahu Schleifer	Anastasia Sobolev
7	**B'Rosh HaShanah** **	Cantor Jill Abramson	Joyce Rosenzweig
8	**Baruch She-amar** *	Cantor Evan Cohen and group	
9	**B'rachah LaCholim (Mi Shebeirach for Healing)** *	Cantor Evan Cohen and group	
10	**Hin'ni He-ani Mima-as** ***	Cantor David Berger	
11	**Hin'ni Ha-aniyah Mima-as (The Female Cantor's Prayer)** *	Cantor Sarah Grabiner	Aya Laipsker-Schleifer
12	**V'ha-eir Eineinu** ***	Cantor David Berger	
13	**V'ha-arev Na** *	Cantor Eliyahu Schleifer	Anastasia Sobolev
14	**V'sham'ru** *	Cantor Evan Cohen	Anastasia Sobolev
15	**Micah, Thus He Said** **	Cantor Galit Dadoun Cohen	Joyce Rosenzweig
16	**Ki Anu Amecha** ****	Cantor Eliyahu Schleifer	Aya Laipsker-Schleifer
17	**Ki Lekach Tov / Eitz Chayim Hi** ****	Cantor Eliyahu Schleifer	Aya Laipsker-Schleifer
18	**Lo Yarei-u** **	Cantor Jill Abramson	Joyce Rosenzweig
19	**Lamdeini Elohai** ****	Cantor Eliyahu Schleifer	Aya Laipsker-Schleifer
20	**Mah Tovu** *	Cantor Sarah Grabiner	Anastasia Sobolev
21	**Mah Nomar L'fanecha** ****	Cantor Eliyahu Schleifer	Aya Laipsker-Schleifer
22	**Modeh / Modah Ani** *	Cantor Evan Cohen	Anastasia Sobolev
23	**Mi Chamochah** *	Cantor Sarah Grabiner	Anastasia Sobolev
24	**K'dushah** **	Cantor Joshua Breitzer with Cantor Galit Dadoun Cohen and Cantor Sam Rosen (responses)	
25	**R'tzeih** *	Cantor Sarah Grabiner	Aya Laipsker-Schleifer
26	**Shehu Noteh Shamayim** **	Cantor Galit Dadoun Cohen	Joyce Rosenzweig
27	**Shehashalom Shelo** **	Cantor Jill Abramson and Cantor Galit Dadoun Cohen	Joyce Rosenzweig

Mizmor L'Eli recordings:
* Produced by Eliyahu Schleifer and Evan Cohen; engineered and mixed by Zvika Hirshler. Recorded in May 2024 at Mishkenot Sha-ananim (Jerusalem, Israel).
** Produced by Joel Eglash; engineered and mixed by Collin Stanley (Mirrortone Studios remote recording) and Joel Eglash. Recorded in May 2024 at Congregation Beit Simchat Torah (New York, New York).
*** Recorded in May 2024 at Transient Sound (Chicago, Illinois).
**** Produced and edited by Doron Schleifer, co-editor Elam Rotem; engineered and mixed by Karl Valter. Recorded in August 2019 at Tonstudio Waldenburg (Waldenburg, Switzerland). Used by permission, with special thanks to Doron Schleifer.

מזמור לאלי
MIZMOR L'ELI

מנגינות-תפילה של אליהו שלייפר
ELIYAHU SCHLEIFER ANTHOLOGY

Ein Kamocha

אין כמוך

Music: **Eliyahu Schleifer**, arr. **Raymond Goldstein**
Text: Torah service liturgy

B
Dm Am Dm C/E Gm6 sus F
in rhythm
nai me-lech, A-do-nai ma-lach, A-do-nai yim-loch l'-o-
E°7 A(sus4) A Gm6 Dm Am Dm C/E
lam va-ed. A-do-nai me-lech, A-do-nai ma-lach, A-do-
Gm6 sus F E°7 A(sus4) A B♭7 C7/B♭
solo
meno mosso
nai yim-loch l'-o-lam va-ed. A-do-nai oz l'-a-
Am/C B♭7 F Gm F Am7 Dm
mo yi-tein, A-do-nai y'-va-reich et a-mo va-sha-lom.
mp

Andante
C
recit.
congregation
Av ha-ra-cha-mim, hei-ti-vah vir-tzon-cha et Tzi-yon, tiv-
neh cho-mot Y'-ru-sha-la-yim. Ki v'-cha l'-vad ba-tach-nu,
Me-lech Eil ram v'-ni-sa, ki v'-cha l'-vad ba-tach-nu,
Me-lech Eil ram v'-ni-sa,
solo
A-
mf
ff

There is none like You among the gods, Adonai,	אֵין כָּמְוֹךָ בָאֱלֹהִים אֲדֹנָי,
and there are no deeds like Yours.	וְאֵין כְּמַעֲשֶׂיךָ.
You are Sovereign over all worlds,	מַלְכוּתְךָ מַלְכוּת כָּל־עֹלָמִים,
and Your dominion is in all generations.	וּמֶמְשַׁלְתְּךָ בְּכָל־דֹּר וָדֹר.
Adonai reigns, Adonai has reigned,	יְיָ מֶלֶךְ, יְיָ מָלָךְ,
Adonai will reign forever and ever.	יְיָ יִמְלֹךְ לְעֹלָם וָעֶד.
Adonai will give strength to our people,	יְיָ עֹז לְעַמּוֹ יִתֵּן,
Adonai will bless our people with peace.	יְיָ יְבָרֵךְ אֶת עַמּוֹ בַשָּׁלוֹם.

Source of mercy:	אַב הָרַחֲמִים,
favor Zion with your goodness;	הֵיטִיבָה בִרְצוֹנְךָ אֶת צִיּוֹן,
rebuild the walls of Jerusalem.	תִּבְנֶה חוֹמוֹת יְרוּשָׁלָיִם.
For in You alone do we trust,	כִּי בְךָ לְבַד בָּטָחְנוּ,
Sovereign, high and exalted, God Eternal.	מֶלֶךְ אֵל רָם וְנִשָּׂא, אֲדוֹן עוֹלָמִים.

Eil Adon

אל אדון

Music: **Eliyahu Schleifer**, arr. **Raymond Goldstein**
Text: Eighth-century rabbinic hymn / Shabbat morning liturgy

Em7 Am7/C Em/B D D F♯m7/C♯ Bm F♯m/A Em/G B7 Em
dar b'-cha - vod al ha-mer-ka-vah, z' - chut u - mi-shor lif - nei chis - o,
D/A A7 D
Meno mosso ♩ = 96
mp
B Bm
che - sed v'-ra - cha-mim lif - nei ch'- vo - do. To - vim m'- o - rot she - ba -
mp legato
F♯7 Bm B7 Em D B7
ra E - lo-hei-nu, y'-tza - ram b'- da - at, b'- vi - nah uv- has - keil. Ko-ach ug-vu-rah na -
Em/B Bm/D Bm/F♯ F♯7 Bm
tan ba - hem, lih' - yot mo-sh-lim b' - ke-rev tei - vel. M' - lei - im ziv um-fi -

F♯7 Bm B7 Em D B7
kim no-gah, na-eh zi-vam b'-chol ha-o-lam. S'-mei-chim b'-tzei-tam v'-sa-
Em Bm/D Bm/F♯ F♯7 Bm
C
D
a tempo
sim b'-vo-am, o-sim b'-ei-mah r'-tzon ko-nam. P'-eir v'-cha-vod no-t-
B A(sus4) A B7 E7 A D
nim lish-mo tzo-ho-lah v'-ri-nah l'-zei-cher mal-chu-to. Ka-ra la-she-mesh v'-
B A7(sus4) A G/A A D
f
F♯m7/C♯ Bm F♯m/A
yiz-rach or, ra-ah v'-hit-kin tzu-rat ha-l'-va-nah. She-vach no-t-

44
Em/G B7 Em Em7 Am7/C Em/B D F♯m7/C♯ Bm F♯m/A
nim___ lo kol___ tz'-va___ ma - rom. Tif - e - ret___
48
Em/G B7 Em D/A mf G/A A7 D
ug - du - lah,___ s'-ra - fim v'-o - fa - nim___ v'-cha - yot___ ha - ko - desh.

God of all creation,
You are blessed with each soul's breath.
Your greatness and goodness fill the world.
Knowledge and understanding surround your glory.
Holiest are You among the holy,
seated in glorious splendor,
radiating purity and justice,
bestowing loving-kindness.
In knowledge and understanding
You created the heavenly lights,
giving them strength and power
to bring light into the world;
full of splendor, they radiate brightness.
The world is warmed by their flames.
We rejoice in their comings and goings,
reflecting the will of their Creator.
Glory and honor they give to You,
glowing praises to Your rule.
You call to the sun and it gives forth light;
You set the patterns of the moon.
You are honored throughout the heavens with songs of glory and praise.
All the heavenly hosts,
give praise, and glory, and honor to God.

אֵל אָדוֹן עַל כָּל הַמַּעֲשִׂים,
בָּרוּךְ וּמְבֹרָךְ בְּפִי כָּל נְשָׁמָה,
גָּדְלוֹ וְטוּבוֹ מָלֵא עוֹלָם,
דַּעַת וּתְבוּנָה סֹבְבִים אוֹתוֹ.
הַמִּתְגָּאֶה עַל חַיּוֹת הַקֹּדֶשׁ,
וְנֶהְדָּר בְּכָבוֹד עַל הַמֶּרְכָּבָה,
זְכוּת וּמִישׁוֹר לִפְנֵי כִסְאוֹ,
חֶסֶד וְרַחֲמִים לִפְנֵי כְבוֹדוֹ.
טוֹבִים מְאוֹרוֹת שֶׁבָּרָא אֱלֹהֵינוּ,
יְצָרָם בְּדַעַת, בְּבִינָה וּבְהַשְׂכֵּל.
כֹּחַ וּגְבוּרָה נָתַן בָּהֶם,
לִהְיוֹת מוֹשְׁלִים בְּקֶרֶב תֵּבֵל.
מְלֵאִים זִיו וּמְפִיקִים נֹגַהּ,
נָאֶה זִיוָם בְּכָל הָעוֹלָם.
שְׂמֵחִים בְּצֵאתָם וְשָׂשִׂים בְּבוֹאָם,
עֹשִׂים בְּאֵימָה רְצוֹן קוֹנָם.
פְּאֵר וְכָבוֹד נוֹתְנִים לִשְׁמוֹ,
צָהֳלָה וְרִנָּה לְזֵכֶר מַלְכוּתוֹ.
קָרָא לַשֶּׁמֶשׁ וַיִּזְרַח אוֹר,
רָאָה וְהִתְקִין צוּרַת הַלְּבָנָה.
שֶׁבַח נוֹתְנִים לוֹ כָּל צְבָא מָרוֹם,
תִּפְאֶרֶת וּגְדֻלָּה,
שְׂרָפִים וְאוֹפַנִּים וְחַיּוֹת הַקֹּדֶשׁ.

Eil Malei Rachamim
(for Yom HaShoah)

אל מלא רחמים
(לנשמות קדושי השואה)

Music and text: Liturgy, ad. **Eliyahu Schleifer**

ram b'-li-bei-nu lo yi - tam. Ba - al ha - ra - cha - mim yas - ti - reim
b' - sei - ter k' - na - fav l' - o - la - mim, v'-yitz - ror bitz -
ror ha - cha - yim et nish - ma - tam A - do - nai hu na - cha - la -
tam. Vi - ku - yam cha - zon ha - na - vi: "Ya - vo sha -
lom ya - nu - chu al mish - k' - vo - tam." V' - no -
mar: "A - mein."

Merciful God, who dwells on high,
protector of widows and father of orphans,
grant true repose
under the wings of the Shechinah,
among the holy and pure righteous ones
who shine like the firmament,
to the souls of millions of our brothers and sisters
who were murdered in the Shoah.
For we and all the House of Israel
pray for the memory of their souls.

May the earth never cover their blood
and may their cry never be silenced.
From generation to generation shall we recall their martyrdom
and their memory shall never end in our hearts.

May the Merciful One shelter them
under the divine protecting wings forever,
and may they dwell
in God's eternal portion.
May the Prophet's vision be fulfilled:
"Peace shall come, and they shall rest wherever they are laid." (After Isaiah 57:2)
And let us say: Amen.

אֵל מָלֵא רַחֲמִים שׁוֹכֵן בַּמְּרוֹמִים,
דַּיַּן אַלְמָנוֹת וַאֲבִי יְתוֹמִים,
הַמְצֵא מְנוּחָה נְכוֹנָה
תַּחַת כַּנְפֵי הַשְּׁכִינָה,
בְּמַעֲלוֹת קְדוֹשִׁים וּטְהוֹרִים
כְּזֹהַר הָרָקִיעַ מַזְהִירִים,
לְנִשְׁמוֹת רִבְבוֹת-אַלְפֵי אַחֵינוּ וְאַחְיוֹתֵינוּ
שֶׁנִּרְצְחוּ בַּשּׁוֹאָה.
בַּעֲבוּר שֶׁאָנוּ וְכָל בֵּית יִשְׂרָאֵל
מִתְפַּלְלִים בְּעַד הַזְכָּרַת נִשְׁמָתָם.

אֶרֶץ אַל תְּכַסִּי דָמָם
וְעַל תִּדְעַךְ זַעֲקָתָם.
לְדוֹר וָדוֹר נַזְכִּיר עֲקֵדָתָם
וְזִכְרָם בְּלִבֵּנוּ לֹא יִתַּם.

בַּעַל הָרַחֲמִים יַסְתִּירֵם
בְּסֵתֶר כְּנָפָיו לְעוֹלָמִים,
וְיִצְרֹר בִּצְרוֹר הַחַיִּים אֶת נִשְׁמָתָם
יְיָ הוּא נַחֲלָתָם.
וִיקֻיַּם חֲזוֹן הַנָּבִיא:
"יָבוֹא שָׁלוֹם יָנוּחוּ עַל מִשְׁכְּבוֹתָם." (ישעיהו נז:ב)
וְנֹאמַר: אָמֵן.

Elohai, N'shamah Shenatata Bi

אלוהי, נשמה שנתת בי

Music: **Eliyahu Schleifer**, arr. **Raymond Goldstein**
Text: Morning liturgy, Birchot Hashachar (Israeli Reform siddur)

For Sarah Pscheidt

B(sus4) B G6 F♯m7(♭5)/C Gmaj7/B
yei o-lam. Kol z' - man she-ha-n'-sha - mah b'-kir -
mf
Allegretto (in rhythm)
A7 Em Em/D♯ Em/D Am
bi, mo - deh a - ni l' - fa - ne - cha, A - do - nai E - lo - hai vEi - lo - hei a - vo - tai, mo-
Em Em/D♯ Em/D Am D7
dah a - ni l' - fa - ne - cha, A - do - nai E - lo - hai vEi - lo - hei i - mo - tai, ri -
rit.
Ped.

G Am A B Cmaj7 Am6 B(omit3)
recit.
bon kol ha-ma-a-sim, a - don kol ha-n'-sha-mot. Ba - ruch a-tah, A-do-nai a -
mp
Em A/E C Em C Am6
rhythmically
rit.
sher b'-ya-do ne - fesh kol chai v'-ru - ach, v'-ru - ach
mf
rit.
Em/B Bm7 Em
a tempo
kol b'-sar ish.

My God, the soul You have given me
is pure.
You created it, You shaped it,
You breathed it into me,
and you protect it within me,
and You will take it from me
to everlasting life.
For as long as my soul is within me,
I offer thanks to You,
Adonai, my God and God of my fathers,
I offer thanks to You,
Adonai, my God and God of my mothers,
Source of all Creation,
Sovereign of all souls.
Praised are You, Adonai,
in whose hand is every living soul
and the breath of every human being.

אֱלֹהַי, נְשָׁמָה שֶׁנָּתַתָּ בִּי
טְהוֹרָה הִיא.
אַתָּה בְרָאתָהּ, אַתָּה יְצַרְתָּהּ,
אַתָּה נְפַחְתָּהּ בִּי,
וְאַתָּה מְשַׁמְּרָהּ בְּקִרְבִּי,
וְאַתָּה עָתִיד לִטְּלָהּ מִמֶּנִּי
לְחַיֵּי עוֹלָם.
כָּל זְמַן שֶׁהַנְּשָׁמָה בְקִרְבִּי,
מוֹדֶה אֲנִי לְפָנֶיךָ,
יְיָ אֱלֹהַי וֵאלֹהֵי אֲבוֹתַי,
מוֹדָה אֲנִי לְפָנֶיךָ,
יְיָ אֱלֹהַי וֵאלֹהֵי אִמּוֹתַי,
רִבּוֹן כָּל הַמַּעֲשִׂים,
אֲדוֹן כָּל הַנְּשָׁמוֹת.
בָּרוּךְ אַתָּה, יְיָ,
אֲשֶׁר בְּיָדוֹ נֶפֶשׁ כָּל חַי
וְרוּחַ כָּל בְּשַׂר-אִישׁ.

Ashreinu

אשרינו

Music: **Eliyahu Schleifer**, arr. **Joyce Rosenzweig**
Text: Morning liturgy (Talmud, *Yoma* 87b)

How happy we are, how good is our portion,
how pleasant our lot, how beautiful our heritage!

אַשְׁרֵינוּ! מַה־טּוֹב חֶלְקֵנוּ,
וּמַה־נָּעִים גּוֹרָלֵנוּ, וּמַה־יָּפָה יְרֻשָּׁתֵנוּ!

Bayom Hahu

ביום הזוא

Music: **Eliyahu Schleifer**
Text: Zechariah 14:9 / End of "Aleinu L'shabei-ach"

Dedicated to Cantor Lori Corrsin

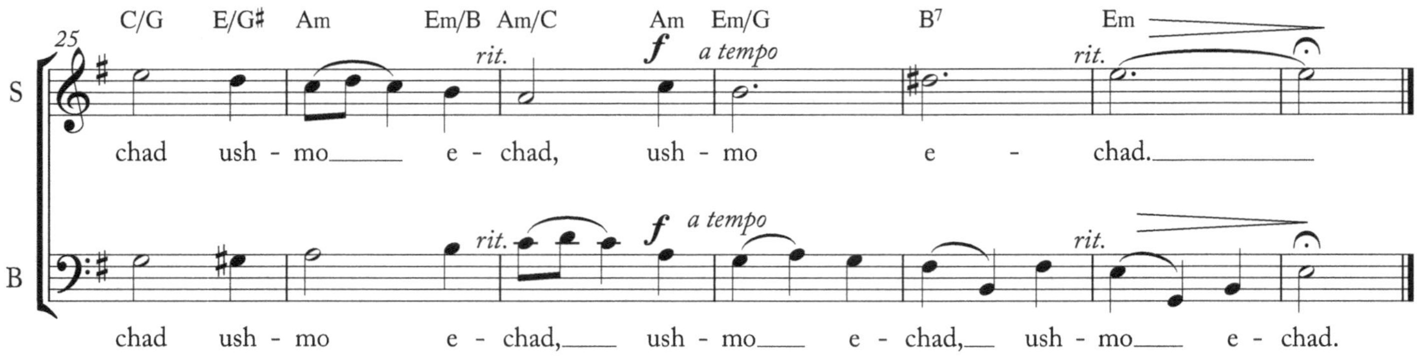

On that day, Adonai will be one,
and God's name will be one.

בַּיּוֹם הַהוּא יִהְיֶה יְיָ אֶחָד
וּשְׁמוֹ אֶחָד.

B'Rosh HaShanah

בראש השנה

Music: **Eliyahu Schleifer**, arr. **Anastasia Sobolev**
Text: High Holy Day liturgy

VERSE 1 recit.
mp lamentoso
p
1. mi yich - yeh, u - mi ya - mut;
p
p
mf
mi v' - ki - tzo, u - mi lo v' - ki - tzo; b' -
D.S.
D.S.
VERSE 2 recit.
f
p
f
p
2. mi va - eish, u - mi va - ma - yim; mi va - che - rev, u -
f
tremolo
p
f

mi va-cha-yah; mi va-ra-av, u - mi va-tza-ma;
misterioso
mi va-ra - - ash, u - mi va-ma-gei-fah; mi va-cha-ni - kah, u-
VERSE 3 recit.
D.S.
mi va - s' - ki-lah; b'- 3. mi ya-nu - ach, u - mi ya - nu - a;

33
p
mf
p
mi yish-a-keit u - mi y'-to-raf; mi yi-sha-leiv, u-
p
36
mf
mi yit - ya-seir; mi ya-a-shir, u - mi ya-a- ni; mi yush -
mf
3
p
p
40
mf
ff
tr
pal, u - mi ya - rum.
3
patetico

congregation:
Utshuvah, utfilah, utzdakah
maavirin et roa hag'zeirah.

On Rosh HaShanah this is written;
on the Fast of Yom Kippur this is sealed:

בְּרֹאשׁ הַשָּׁנָה יִכָּתֵבוּן,
וּבְיוֹם צוֹם כִּפּוּר יֵחָתֵמוּן:

How many will pass away from this world,
how many will be born into it;
who will live and who will die;
who will reach the ripeness of age,
who will be taken before their time;
who by fire and who by water;
who by war and who by beast;
who by famine and who by drought;
who by earthquake and who by plague;
who by strangling and who by stoning;
who will rest and who will wander;
who will be tranquil and who will be troubled;
who will be calm and who tormented;
who will live in prosperity and who in poverty;
who will be humbled and who exalted—

כַּמָּה יַעֲבֹרוּן,
וְכַמָּה יִבָּרֵאוּן.
מִי יִחְיֶה, וּמִי יָמוּת.
מִי בְקִצּוֹ,
וּמִי לֹא בְקִצּוֹ.
מִי בָאֵשׁ, וּמִי בַמַּיִם.
מִי בַחֶרֶב, וּמִי בַחַיָּה.
מִי בָרָעָב, וּמִי בַצָּמָא.
מִי בָרַעַשׁ, וּמִי בַמַּגֵּפָה.
מִי בַחֲנִיקָה, וּמִי בַסְּקִילָה.
מִי יָנוּחַ, וּמִי יָנוּעַ.
מִי יִשָּׁקֵט, וּמִי יְטֹּרֵף.
מִי יִשָּׁלֵו, וּמִי יִתְיַסֵּר.
מִי יַעֲשִׁיר, וּמִי יַעֲנִי.
מִי יֵשְׁפַּל, וּמִי יָרוּם —

But through return to the right path, through prayer and righteousness,
we can transcend the harshness of the decree.

וּתְשׁוּבָה, וּתְפִלָּה, וּצְדָקָה
מַעֲבִירִין אֶת רֹעַ הַגְּזֵרָה.

Baruch She-amar

ברוך שאמר

Music: **Eliyahu Schleifer**, according to Shabbat *nusach*
Text: Morning liturgy (Israeli Reform siddur)

Dedicated to Cantor Evan Cohen

B
29
mf
ruch ma-a-vir a-fei-lah u-me-vi o-rah, o-rah, ba-
33
f
ruch sh'-mo. Ba-ruch chai la-ad v'-ka-yam la-
38
ne-tzach, ba-ruch hu. Ba-ruch po-deh
42
u-ma-tzil, ba-ruch hu u-va-ruch sh'-mo.
C recitative
Ba-ruch a-tah, A-do-
46
nai, E-lo-hei-nu Me-lech ha-o-lam, ha-Eil ha-av ha-ra-cha-
50
man, ham'-hu-lal b'-fi a-mo, m'-shu-bach um-fo-
54
ar bil-shon cha-si-dav va-a-va-dav. Ba-
57
optional ending
ruch A-tah, A-do-nai, Me-lech m'-hu-lal ba-tish-ba-chot.
ruch a-tah, A-do-nai, Me-lech m'-hu-lal ba-tish-ba-chot.

Blessed is the One who spoke and the world came to be.	בָּרוּךְ שֶׁאָמַר וְהָיָה הָעוֹלָם,
Blessed is the One!	בָּרוּךְ הוּא.
Blessed is the One who continually authors creation.	בָּרוּךְ עוֹשֶׂה בְרֵאשִׁית,
Blessed is God's name!	בָּרוּךְ שְׁמוֹ.
Blessed is the One whose word is deed.	בָּרוּךְ אוֹמֵר וְעוֹשֶׂה,
Blessed is the One!	בָּרוּךְ הוּא.
Blessed is the One who decrees and fulfills.	בָּרוּךְ גּוֹזֵר וּמְקַיֵּם,
Blessed is God's name!	בָּרוּךְ שְׁמוֹ.
Blessed is the One who is compassionate toward the world.	בָּרוּךְ מְרַחֵם עַל הָאָרֶץ,
Blessed is the One!	בָּרוּךְ הוּא.
Blessed is the One who is compassionate toward all creatures.	בָּרוּךְ מְרַחֵם עַל הַבְּרִיוֹת,
Blessed is God's name!	בָּרוּךְ שְׁמוֹ.
Blessed is the One who rewards the reverent.	בָּרוּךְ מְשַׁלֵּם שָׂכָר טוֹב לִירֵאָיו,
Blessed is the One!	בָּרוּךְ הוּא.
Blessed is the One who removes the darkness and brings light.	בָּרוּךְ מַעֲבִיר אֲפֵלָה וּמֵבִיא אוֹרָה,
Blessed is God's name!	בָּרוּךְ שְׁמוֹ.
Blessed is the One who exists for all time, ever-enduring.	בָּרוּךְ חַי לָעַד וְקַיָּם לָנֶצַח,
Blessed is the One!	בָּרוּךְ הוּא.
Blessed is the One who redeems and saves.	בָּרוּךְ פּוֹדֶה וּמַצִּיל,
Blessed is God and blessed is God's name!	בָּרוּךְ הוּא וּבָרוּךְ שְׁמוֹ.
Blessed are You, Adonai,	בָּרוּךְ אַתָּה, יְיָ,
Sovereign of time and space,	אֱלֹהֵינוּ מֶלֶךְ הָעוֹלָם,
compassionate Creator,	הָאֵל הָאָב הָרַחֲמָן,
celebrated in Your people's voices,	הַמְהֻלָּל בְּפִי עַמּוֹ,
praised and glorified by the words	מְשֻׁבָּח וּמְפֹאָר בִּלְשׁוֹן
of Your faithful servants,	חֲסִידָיו וַעֲבָדָיו.
Blessed are You, Adonai,	בָּרוּךְ אַתָּה, יְיָ,
Sovereign who is glorified through praise.	מֶלֶךְ מְהֻלָּל בַּתִּשְׁבָּחוֹת.

B'rachah LaCholim

Mi Shebeirach for Healing

ברכה לחולים

מי שברך לרפואה

Music: **Eliyahu Schleifer**
Text: Compiled by **Eliyahu Schleifer**

Dedicated to Rabbi Ada Zavidov and Cantor Evan Cohen

Alternatively, the rabbi may begin by reciting a different prayer and reading the names.
Then, the cantor may follow by humming section B and then singing sections A and C (as done at Kehilat Har-El in Jerusalem).

ברכה לחולים (מי שברך לרפואה)

B'rachah LaCholim
(Mi Shebeirach for Healing)

May the One who blessed our fathers,
Abraham, Isaac and Jacob,
may the One who blessed our mothers,
Sarah, Rebecca, Rachel, and Leah,
bless all in need of healing.

God, I pray, heal her.
God, I pray, heal him.
God, I pray, heal them,
with complete recovery.

מִי שֶׁבֵּרַךְ אֲבוֹתֵינוּ,
אַבְרָהָם, יִצְחָק, וְיַעֲקֹב,
מִי שֶׁבֵּרַךְ אִמּוֹתֵינוּ,
שָׂרָה, רִבְקָה, רָחֵל, וְלֵאָה,
הוּא יְבָרֵךְ וִירַפֵּא אֶת הַחוֹלִים.

אֵל נָא רְפָא נָא לָהּ.
אֵל נָא רְפָא נָא לוֹ.
אֵל נָא רְפָא נָא לָהֶם,
רְפוּאָה שְׁלֵמָה.

Hin'ni He-ani Mimaas הנני העני ממעש

Music: **Eliyahu Schleifer**
Text: High Holy Day liturgy

In tempo ♩ = 76
yom v'-no-ra, he-yei na matz-li-ach dar-ki a-
meno mosso rubato
sher a-no-chi ho-leich la-a-mod ul-va-keish ra-cha-mim a-
rit.
agitato
lai v'-al sho-l'-chai. Na al taf-shi-eim b'-cha-to-tai, v'-
rit.
al t'-cha-y'-veim ba-a-vo-no-tai, ki cho-tei u-fo-shei-a a-ni. V'-
agitato
al yi-ka-l'-mu bif-sha-ai v'-al yei-vo-shu heim bi v'-al ei-
vosh a-ni ba-hem. Ka-beil, ka-beil t'-fi-la-
ti kit-fi-lat za-kein, za-kein v'-ra-gil u-fir-ko na-eh, uz-ka-
no m'-gu-dal, v'-ko-lo na-im, u-m'-o-
rav b'-da-at im ha-b'-ri-yot. V'-tig-ar ba-Sa-

with ugly voice
In tempo ♩ = 76
52
tan l'-val yas-ti-nei-ni. Vi-hi na di-lu-gei-nu a-
56
free recit.
le-cha a-ha-vah, vi-hi na di-lu-gei-nu a-le-cha a-ha-vah, v'-al kol p'-sha-
59
im t'-cha-seh b'-a-ha-vah. Kol tza-rot, tza-
62
rit.
rot v'-ra-ot ha-foch na la-nu ul-chol Yis-ra-el l'-
In tempo ♩ = 76
65
sa-son ul-sim-chah, l'-cha-yim ul-sha-lom, l'-sa-son ul-sim-chah, l'-
68
free recit.
cha-yim ul-sha-lom. Ha-e-met v'-ha-sha-lom e-ha-vu, v'-
70
whisper softly
lo y'-hi shum mich-shol bit-fi-la-ti. Vi-hi ra-
73
tzon mi-l'-fa-ne-cha, A-do-nai, E-lo-hei Av-ra-ham, E-lo-hei Yitz-chak, vEi-lo-hei Ya-a-
76
Reform text insert
kov, E-lo-hei Sa-rah, E-lo-hei Riv-kah, E-lo-hei Ra-cheil vEi-lo-hei Lei-

* Based on the melody of Rebbe Yitzchak Ayzik of Kalib's song "Szól A Kokos Már" ("The Rooster's Cry"), which became the anthem of Hungarian Jews. It is used here as a symbol for the martyrs of the Shoah.

Poor in worthy deeds,
I am horribly frightened in Your presence,
who are enthroned and receiving praise from Israel.
I have come to plead before You
on behalf of Your people Israel,
who have made me messenger though I am not deserving nor qualified for the

הִנְנִי הֶעָנִי מִמַּעַשׂ,
נִרְעָשׁ וְנִפְחָד מִפַּחַד
יוֹשֵׁב תְּהִלּוֹת יִשְׂרָאֵל.
בָּאתִי לַעֲמֹד וּלְהִתְחַנֵּן לְפָנֶיךָ
עַל עַמְּךָ יִשְׂרָאֵל אֲשֶׁר שְׁלָחוּנִי,
אַף עַל פִּי שֶׁאֵינִי כְּדַאי וְהָגוּן לְכָךְ.

Hence I beseech You,
God of Abraham and Isaac and Jacob,
God of Sarah, Rebecca, Rachel, and Leah,
O God, merciful and gracious God of Israel,
almighty and revered One,
make my errand successful when I seek mercy for myself
and for those who have commissioned me.

לָכֵן אֲבַקֵּשׁ מִמְּךָ,
אֱלֹהֵי אַבְרָהָם, אֱלֹהֵי יִצְחָק, וֵאלֹהֵי יַעֲקֹב,
אֱלֹהֵי שָׂרָה, אֱלֹהֵי רִבְקָה, וֵאלֹהֵי רָחֵל וְלֵאָה,
יְיָ, יְיָ, אֵל רַחוּם וְחַנּוּן, אֱלֹהֵי יִשְׂרָאֵל,
שַׁדַּי אָיוֹם וְנוֹרָא,
הֱיֵה נָא מַצְלִיחַ דַּרְכִּי אֲשֶׁר אָנוֹכִי הוֹלֵךְ
לַעֲמוֹד וּלְבַקֵּשׁ רַחֲמִים עָלַי וְעַל שׁוֹלְחָי.

Blame them not for my sins,
convict them not for my iniquities,
for I am a transgressor indeed.
Let them not be shamed
because of me and my faults,
nor let me be shamed because of them.

נָא אַל תַּפְשִׁיעֵם בְּחַטֹּאתַי,
וְעַל תְּחַיְּבֵם בַּעֲוֹנֹתַי,
כִּי חוֹטֵא וּפוֹשֵׁעַ אָנִי.
וְאַל יִכָּלְמוּ בִּפְשָׁעַי
וְאַל יֵבוֹשׁוּ הֵם בִּי
וְאַל אֵבוֹשׁ אֲנִי בָּהֶם.

Accept my prayer as if I were a qualified and well-versed messenger,
whose reputation is umblemished, his beard long, and his voice sweet,
and who is loved by his fellow human beings.

קַבֵּל תְּפִלָּתִי כִּתְפִלַּת זָקֵן וְרָגִיל,
וּפִרְקוֹ נָאֶה, וּזְקָנוֹ מְגֻדָּל, וְקוֹלוֹ נָעִים,
וּמְעֹרָב בְּדַעַת עִם הַבְּרִיּוֹת.

Rebuke the adversary, that he may not accuse me,
accept our prayers with love,
and by Your love, may You hide all our transgressions.

וְתִגְעַר בַּשָּׂטָן לְבַל יַשְׂטִינֵנִי.
וִיהִי נָא דִלּוּגֵנוּ עָלֶיךָ אַהֲבָה,
וְעַל כָּל פְּשָׁעִים תְּכַסֶּה בְּאַהֲבָה.

Turn all our troubles and afflictions
and those of all Israel
into joy and gladness, life and peace.

כָּל צָרוֹת וְרָעוֹת
הֲפָךְ־נָא לָנוּ וּלְכָל יִשְׂרָאֵל,
לְשָׂשׂוֹן וּלְשִׂמְחָה, לְחַיִּים וּלְשָׁלוֹם.

May we love the truth and peace,
and may no obstruction impede my prayer.

הָאֱמֶת וְהַשָּׁלוֹם אֱהָבוּ,
וְלֹא יְהִי שׁוּם מִכְשׁוֹל בִּתְפִלָּתִי.

O God,
God of Abraham and Isaac and Jacob
God of Sarah, Rebecca, Leah, and Rachel,
who is the revered most high and eternal God,
may it be Your will

וִיהִי רָצוֹן מִלְּפָנֶיךָ, יְיָ,
אֱלֹהֵי אַבְרָהָם, אֱלֹהֵי יִצְחָק, וֵאלֹהֵי יַעֲקֹב,
אֱלֹהֵי שָׂרָה, אֱלֹהֵי רִבְקָה, וֵאלֹהֵי רָחֵל וְלֵאָה,
הָאֵל הַגָּדוֹל הַגִּבּוֹר וְהַנּוֹרָא,
אֵל עֶלְיוֹן, אֶהְיֶה אֲשֶׁר אֶהְיֶה,

Reform Version—
that my prayer ascend
to Your glorious throne,

שֶׁתָּבוֹא תְּפִלָּתִי
לִפְנֵי כִּסֵּא כְבוֹדֶךָ,

Traditional Version—
that all the interceding angels
convey my prayer
before Your glorious throne
and present it to You,

שֶׁכָּל הַמַּלְאָכִים שֶׁהֵם מַעֲלֵי תְּפִלּוֹת
יָבִיאוּ תְּפִלָּתִי
לִפְנֵי כִּסֵּא כְבוֹדֶךָ,
וְיַצִּיגוּ אוֹתָהּ לְפָנֶיךָ,

All Versions—
in the name of all upright
and honest persons,
and for the sake of Your own glorious and revered name,
for You hear the prayers of Israel Your people
in mercy.
Blessed are You, who hears prayer.

בַּעֲבוּר כָּל הַצַּדִּיקִים וְהַחֲסִידִים,
הַתְּמִימִים וְהַיְשָׁרִים,
וּבַעֲבוּר כְּבוֹד שִׁמְךָ הַגָּדוֹל וְהַנּוֹרָא,
כִּי אַתָּה שׁוֹמֵעַ תְּפִלַּת עַמְּךָ יִשְׂרָאֵל
בְּרַחֲמִים.
בָּרוּךְ אַתָּה, שׁוֹמֵעַ תְּפִלָּה.

Hin'ni Ha-aniyah Mima-as הנני העניה ממעש

The Female Cantor's Prayer

Music: **Eliyahu Schleifer**, arr. **Doron Schleifer**
Text: High Holy Day liturgy, feminine text by **Eliyahu Schleifer**

Dedicated to Cantor Sarah Grabiner

994058

11
nein l' - fa - ne - cha al a - m'-cha Yis - ra - el a -
13
f
rit.
mp
sher sh'-la - chu - ni, af al pi she-ei-ni ch'-da-
rit.
17
p
it she-ei-ni ch'-da-it u - r' - u-yah l' - chach.
20
mp
B
La - chein, la - chein a - va-keish mi - m'-cha, E - lo -

22
hei Av-ra-ham, E-lo-hei Yitz-chak, vEi-lo-hei Ya - a - kov, E-lo-
24
hei Sa-rah, E-lo-hei Riv-kah, vEi-lo-hei Ra-cheil v'-Lei - ah, A-do-
mp
27
nai, A - do-nai, Eil ra - chum v' - cha-nun E-lo-hei Yis-ra-
29
f
el, Sha-dai a - yom v'-no-ra, he-
mp

In tempo ♩ = 76
yei na matz-li-ach dar-ki a - sher a-no-chi ho - le - chet la - a-
meno mosso rubato
rit.
mod, l' - va - keish ra - cha-mim a - lai v' - al sho - l'-
C
agitato
chai. Na al taf - shi - eim b' - cha - to - tai, v' -
rit.
al t'-cha-y'-veim ba - a - vo - no - tai, ki cho - teit u - fo - sha - at a - ni.

42
mf
agitato
mp
V' - al yi-ka-l'-mu bif-sha - ai v' - al yei-vo-shu heim
45
mp
bi v'-al ei - vosh a-ni ba-hem. Ka-
D
49
beil t' - fi - la - ti kit - fi - lat Cha - nah u - ch - shi -
52
rat Mir-yam u-Dvo - rah, v - et - ya -

tzeiv l'-fa-ne-cha kish-lu-chat a-m'-cha beit Yis-ra-el, she-d'-va-
re-ha a-rei-vim v'-ko-lah na-im, u-m'-o-
re-vet b'-da-at im ha-b'-ri-yot. V'-tig-ar ba-Sa-
tan l'-val yas-ti-nei-ni. Vi-
E
mf
f

In Tempo ♩ = 76
like a Chasidic dance
mp
67
hi na dig-lei - nu a - le - cha a - ha - vah, vi -
69
free recit.
hi na dig-lei - nu a-le-cha a - ha - vah, v'-al kol p'-sha-im
3
3
71
6
t'-cha-seh b'-a-ha-vah.
p
F
75
mp
p
3
6
Kol tza-rot, tza - rot v'-ra-ot ha-foch la-nu

In Tempo ♩ = 76
rit.
rit.
f
ul - chol Yis-ra - el l' - sa - son ul - sim - chah, l' -
cha - yim ul - sha - lom, l' - sa - son ul - sim - chah, l' -
cha - yim ul - sha - lom,

l' - sa - son ul' - sim - chah. l' -
free recit.
cha - yim ul - sha - lom. Ha - e - met v'-ha-sha-lom e - ha - vu, v' - lo y' - hi
shum mich - shol bit - fi - la - ti.

Silent Prayer
rit.
mf
G
Ki a - tah
rit.
f
mp
sho-mei - a t'-fi-lat a-m'-cha Yis-ra-el b'-ra-cha-mim. Ba-ruch a -
tah, sho-mei - a t'-fi - lah.
pp

Poor in worthy deed,
I am excited and frightened in Your presence,
O God, who are enthroned by the praises of Israel.
I have come to stand before You and plead
on behalf of Your people Israel, who have made me their messenger,
though I am not deserving and worthy of the task.

הִנְנִי הָעֲנִיָּה מִמַּעַשׂ,
נִרְעֶשֶׁת וְנִפְחֶדֶת מִפַּחַד
יוֹשֵׁב תְּהִלּוֹת יִשְׂרָאֵל.
בָּאתִי לַעֲמֹד וּלְהִתְחַנֵּן לְפָנֶיךָ
עַל עַמְּךָ יִשְׂרָאֵל אֲשֶׁר שְׁלָחוּנִי,
אַף עַל פִּי שֶׁאֵינִי כְדָאִית וּרְאוּיָה לְכָךְ.

Therefore, I beseech You,
God of Abraham, Isaac, and Jacob,
God of Sarah, Rebecca, Rachel, and Leah.
Adonai, Adonai, merciful and gracious, God of Israel,
almighty and awesome one,
make my way successful, as I proceed to seek mercy for myself
and for those who commissioned me.

לָכֵן אֲבַקֵּשׁ מִמְּךָ,
אֱלֹהֵי אַבְרָהָם, אֱלֹהֵי יִצְחָק, וֵאלֹהֵי יַעֲקֹב,
אֱלֹהֵי שָׂרָה, אֱלֹהֵי רִבְקָה, וֵאלֹהֵי רָחֵל וְלֵאָה,
יְיָ, יְיָ, אֵל רַחוּם וְחַנּוּן אֱלֹהֵי יִשְׂרָאֵל,
שַׁדַּי אָיוֹם וְנוֹרָא,
הֱיֵה נָא מַצְלִיחַ דַּרְכִּי אֲשֶׁר אָנֹכִי הוֹלֶכֶת
לַעֲמוֹד לְבַקֵּשׁ רַחֲמִים עָלַי וְעַל שׁוֹלְחַי.

Please do not blame them for my sins,
and do not convict them for my transgressions,
for I am indeed a sinner and transgressor.
Let them not be ashamed because of my faults,
nor let me be ashamed
because of them.

נָא אַל תַּפְשִׁיעֵם בְּחַטֹּאתַי,
וְעַל תְּחַיְּבֵם בַּעֲוֹנֹתַי,
כִּי חוֹטֵאת וּפוֹשַׁעַת אָנִי.
וְאַל יִכָּלְמוּ בִּפְשָׁעַי
וְאַל יֵבוֹשׁוּ הֵם בִּי
וְאַל אֵבוֹשׁ אֲנִי בָּהֶם.

Accept my prayer like the prayer of Hannah
and the songs of Miriam and Deborah,
and may I stand before You as the advocate of Your people Israel,
a messenger whose words are pleasant, her voice is sweet,
and she is at one mind with her people.

קַבֵּל תְּפִלָּתִי כִּתְפִלַּת חַנָּה
וּכְשִׁירַת מִרְיָם וּדְבוֹרָה,
וְאֶתְיַצֵּב לְפָנֶיךָ כִּשְׁלוּחַת עַמְּךָ בֵּית יִשְׂרָאֵל,
שֶׁדְּבָרֶיהָ עֲרֵבִים וְקוֹלָהּ נָעִים
וּמְעֹרֶבֶת בְּדַעַת עִם הַבְּרִיּוֹת.

Rebuke the adversary that he may not accuse me.
May our relations with You be of love,
and may all our sins be pardoned by Your love.
Turn our afflictions and troubles and those of all Israel
to joy and gladness, to life and peace.
"Love truth and peace,"
let my prayer be without stumbling.

וְתִגְעַר בַּשָּׂטָן לְבַל יַשְׂטִינֵנִי.
וִיהִי נָא דִּגְלֵנוּ עָלֶיךָ אַהֲבָה,
וְעַל כָּל פְּשָׁעִים תְּכַסֶּה בְּאַהֲבָה.
כָּל צָרוֹת וְרָעוֹת הֲפֹךְ לָנוּ וּלְכָל יִשְׂרָאֵל
לְשָׂשׂוֹן וּלְשִׂמְחָה, לְחַיִּים וּלְשָׁלוֹם.
"הָאֱמֶת וְהַשָּׁלוֹם אֱהָבוּ",
וְלֹא יְהִי שׁוּם מִכְשׁוֹל בִּתְפִלָּתִי.

For You hear the prayer of Your people Israel with mercy.
Blessed are You, who hears prayer.

כִּי אַתָּה שׁוֹמֵעַ תְּפִלַּת עַמְּךָ יִשְׂרָאֵל בְּרַחֲמִים.
בָּרוּךְ אַתָּה, שׁוֹמֵעַ תְּפִלָּה.

V'ha-eir Eineinu

והאר עינינו

Music: **Eliyahu Schleifer**
Text: Morning liturgy

Enlighten our eyes with Your Torah,
focus our minds on Your mitzvot,
unite our hearts in love
and reverence for Your name.
Then we will never feel shame,
never deserve rebuke, and never stumble.
Having trusted in Your great and awesome holiness,
we shall celebrate Your salavation with joy.
Gather us in peace from the four corners of the earth
and lead us upright to our land.
For You, O God, work wonders.
You chose us. Truly, You drew us near to Your great name,
that we might acknowledge You, declaring You One in love.
Praised be You, Adonai,
who chooses Your people Israel in love.

וְהָאֵר עֵינֵינוּ בְּתוֹרָתֶךָ,
וְדַבֵּק לִבֵּנוּ בְּמִצְוֹתֶיךָ,
וְיַחֵד לְבָבֵנוּ לְאַהֲבָה
וּלְיִרְאָה אֶת־שְׁמֶךָ,
וְלֹא נֵבוֹשׁ וְלֹא נִכָּלֵם,
וְלֹא נִכָּשֵׁל לְעוֹלָם וָעֶד.
כִּי בְשֵׁם קָדְשְׁךָ הַגָּדוֹל וְהַנּוֹרָא בָּטָחְנוּ,
נָגִילָה וְנִשְׂמְחָה בִּישׁוּעָתֶךָ.
וַהֲבִיאֵנוּ לְשָׁלוֹם מֵאַרְבַּע כַּנְפוֹת הָאָרֶץ,
וְתוֹלִיכֵנוּ קוֹמְמִיּוּת לְאַרְצֵנוּ.
כִּי אֵל פּוֹעֵל יְשׁוּעוֹת אָתָּה, וּבָנוּ בָחַרְתָּ
וְקֵרַבְתָּנוּ לְשִׁמְךָ הַגָּדוֹל סֶלָה בֶּאֱמֶת,
לְהוֹדוֹת לְךָ וּלְיַחֶדְךָ בְּאַהֲבָה.
בָּרוּךְ אַתָּה, יְיָ,
הַבּוֹחֵר בְּעַמּוֹ יִשְׂרָאֵל בְּאַהֲבָה.

V'ha-arev Na

והערב נא

Music: **Eliyahu Schleifer**
Text: Weekday morning liturgy

Dedicated to the blessed memory of Rabbi Dr. David Ellenson

Blessed are You, Adonai our God,
Sovereign of the universe,
who hallows us with mitzvot,
commanding us to engage with words of Torah.

בָּרוּךְ אַתָּה, יְיָ,
אֱלֹהֵינוּ מֶלֶךְ הָעוֹלָם,
אֲשֶׁר קִדְּשָׁנוּ בְּמִצְוֹתָיו
וְצִוָּנוּ לַעֲסוֹק בְּדִבְרֵי תוֹרָה.

O Adonai, our God,
let the words of Torah be sweet in our mouths,
so that we, our descendants
and the descendants of all Your people Israel
may know You,
by studying your Torah for its own sake.
Blessed are You, Adonai,
who teaches Torah to Your people Israel.

וְהַעֲרֶב־נָא יְיָ אֱלֹהֵינוּ
אֶת־דִּבְרֵי תוֹרָתְךָ בְּפִינוּ,
וְנִהְיֶה אֲנַחְנוּ וְצֶאֱצָאֵינוּ,
וְצֶאֱצָאֵי עַמְּךָ בֵּית יִשְׂרָאֵל,
כֻּלָּנוּ יוֹדְעֵי שְׁמֶךָ,
וְלוֹמְדֵי תוֹרָתֶךָ לִשְׁמָהּ.
בָּרוּךְ אַתָּה, יְיָ,
הַמְלַמֵּד תּוֹרָה לְעַמּוֹ יִשְׂרָאֵל.

V'sham'ru ושמרו

Music: **Eliyahu Schleifer**, arr. **Anastasia Sobolev**
Text: Exodus 31:16-17 / Shabbat morning *Kiddush*

B
G G/F♯ Em7 G Cmaj7 Bm A7 D Em
mp
13
Bei - ni u-vein b'-nei Yis-ra - el ot hi l'-o - lam, ki
dolce
Am Em C A♯o B(sus4) B
17
rit.
mf
shei-shet ya-mim a-sah A-do-nai et ha-sha-ma-yim v'-et ha-a - retz,
semplice
rit.
a tempo
C
Em D Em D Cmaj7 D Em7 Bm7 Em
21
mp
u - va - yom ha-sh'-vi - i sha - vat va-yi - na - fash,
mp
a tempo

The people of Israel
shall keep Shabbat,
observing Shabbat throughtout the ages
as a covenant for all time.
It is a sign for all time between Me and the people of Israel,
for in six days Adonai
made heaven and earth,
and on the seventh day
God ceased from work and was refreshed.

וְשָׁמְרוּ בְנֵי יִשְׂרָאֵל
אֶת-הַשַּׁבָּת,
לַעֲשׂוֹת אֶת-הַשַּׁבָּת לְדֹרֹתָם
בְּרִית עוֹלָם.
בֵּינִי וּבֵין בְּנֵי יִשְׂרָאֵל
אוֹת הִיא לְעוֹלָם,
כִּי-שֵׁשֶׁת יָמִים עָשָׂה יְיָ
אֶת-הַשָּׁמַיִם וְאֶת-הָאָרֶץ,
וּבַיּוֹם הַשְּׁבִיעִי שָׁבַת וַיִּנָּפַשׁ.

Micah, Thus He Said

כֹּה אָמַר מִיכָה

Music: **Eliyahu Schleifer**, arr. **Anastasia Sobolev**
Text: Based upon the Book of Micah 6:6-8

down before God on high? Should I come before God with
burnt offerings, with yearling calves? Would the Eternal be
pleased with thousands of rams, with ten thousand rivers of
oil? Should I give my firstborn for my transgressions, the fruit of my
B
sub. p

weeping voice
bod - y for my own sin?" The spir - it of God was up - on
Mi - cah, and Mi - cah de - clared: "He has told you, O mor - tal, what is
good and what the E - ter - nal re - qui - res of you: On - ly to do
C ♩ = ca. 76
just - ly, and love mer - cy, and walk humb - ly with your God, on -
1.

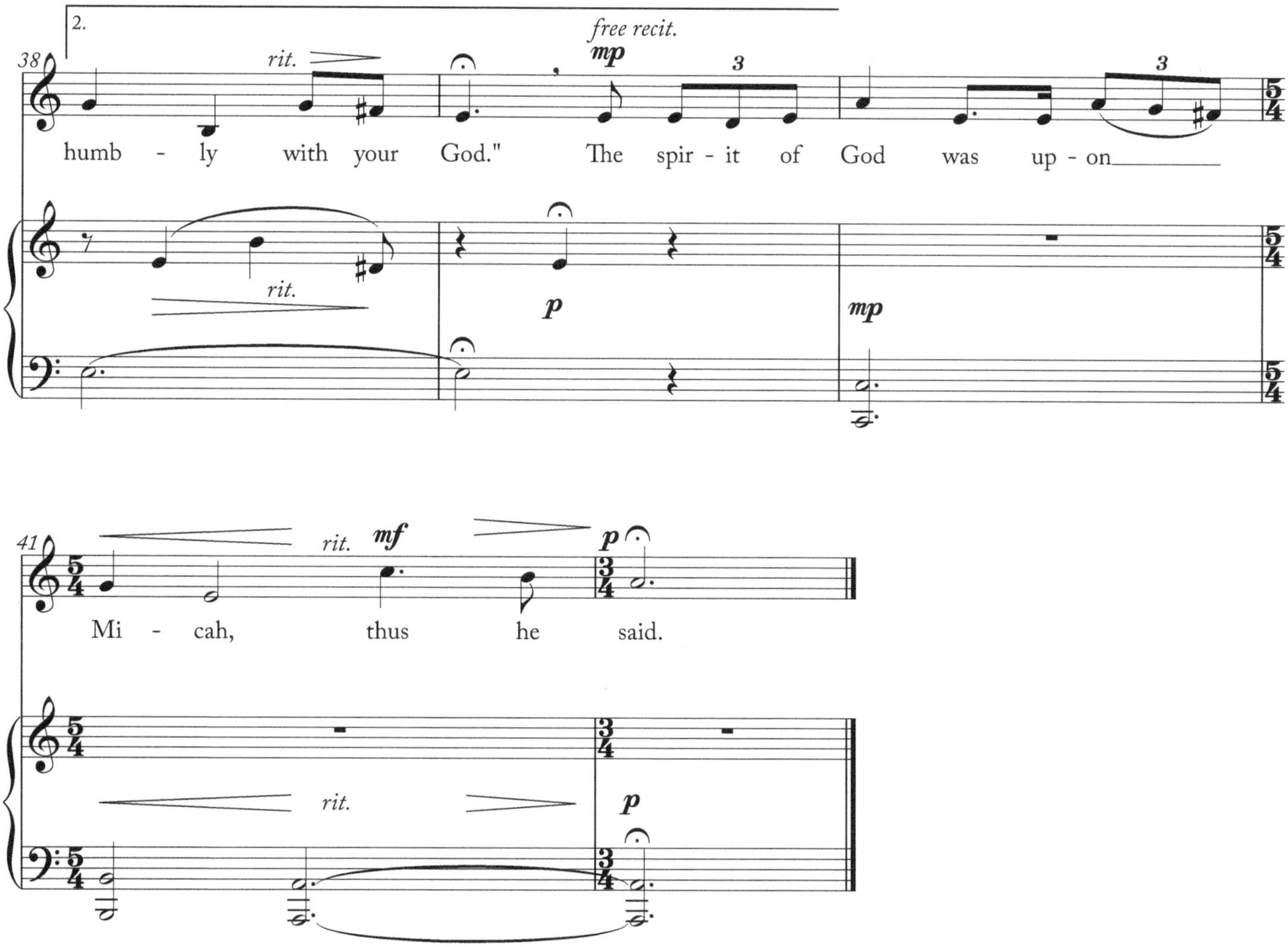

The spirit of God was upon Micah, and Micah asked:
"With what should I come to the Eternal
and bow down before God on high?
Should I come before God with burnt offerings,
with yearling calves?
Would the Eternal be pleased with thousands of rams,
with ten thousand rivers of oil?
Should I give my firstborn for my transgression,
the fruit of my body for my own sin?"
The spirit of God was upon Micah, and Micah declared:
"He has told you, O mortal, what is good
and what the Eternal requires of you:
Only to do justly, and love mercy,
and walk humbly with your God."
The spirit of God was upon Micah,
thus he said.

Ki Anu Amecha

כי אנו עמך

Music: **Eliyahu Schleifer** / Traditional, arr. **Doron Schleifer**
Text: High Holy Day liturgy (*Gates of Repentance*)

For Marcy Kadin

B
a - nu a - me - cha, v'-a - tah mal - kei -
Ped.
nu, a - nu va - ne - cha, v'-a-
tah a - vi - - nu. A - nu na - cha-la-
mf
te - cha, v'-a - tah go - ra - lei - nu;

24
mf
f
a - nu tzo - ne - cha, v'-a - tah ro - ei -
27
mf
nu. A - nu char - me - cha, v'-a-
30
mp
tah not - rei - nu; a - nu ra - ya-
33
Last time to Coda
te - cha, v'-a - tah do - dei - nu.
Last time to Coda

Freely
C
We are Your peo- ple, You are our King; we are Your chil- dren, You are our fa- ther;
we are Your pos- ses- sion, You are our por- tion; we are Your flock, You are our shep - herd;
we are Your vine- yard, You are our keep- er; we are Your be- lo - ved, You are our friend.
rit.
D.S. al Coda
CODA
falsetto
tah do- dei - nu.
p
pp

אֱלֹהֵינוּ וֵאלֹהֵי אֲבוֹתֵינוּ וְאִמּוֹתֵינוּ,
סְלַח לָנוּ, מְחַל לָנוּ, כַּפֶּר־לָנוּ.

כִּי אָנוּ עַמֶּךָ, וְאַתָּה מַלְכֵּנוּ,
אָנוּ בָנֶיךָ, וְאַתָּה אָבִינוּ.
אָנוּ נַחֲלָתֶךָ, וְאַתָּה גוֹרָלֵנוּ,
אָנוּ צֹאנֶךָ, וְאַתָּה רוֹעֵנוּ.
אָנוּ כַרְמֶךָ, וְאַתָּה נוֹטְרֵנוּ,
אָנוּ רַעְיָתֶךָ, וְאַתָּה דוֹדֵנוּ.

Our God and God of all generations,
forgive us, pardon us, lead us to atonement.

We are Your people, You are our God.
We are Your children, You are our father.
We are Your possession, You are our purpose.
We are Your flock, You are our shepherd.
We are Your vineyard, You are our keeper.
We are Your beloved, You are our friend.

English translation from *Gates of Repentance*

Ki Lekach Tov / Eitz Chayim Hi

כי לקח טוב / עץ חיים היא

Music: **Eliyahu Schleifer**, arr. **Raymond Goldstein**

Text: Proverbs 4:2, 3:18, 3:17; Lamentations 5:21 / Torah service

Dedicated to pianist Joyce Rosenzweig

Fmaj7 G Fmaj7/A Em7 D Dm A(sus4) Am
13
che - ha m'-u - shar. D'-ra - che-ha dar-chei no - am, v'-
B°7/F E(sus4) Em Dm Fmaj7/C E(sus4) Fmaj7
17
chol n'-ti-vo-te-ha sha-lom, d'-ra - che-ha dar-chei no - am, v'-
N.C. Dm Dm7 1. A(sus4) Am 2. A(sus4) Am
21
solo and congregation mf
chol n'-ti-vo-te-ha sha - lom. Eitz cha-yim lom.
B°7/F Dm9 E7(omit3) Fmaj7 Dm E7(omit3) A(sus4) Am
24
mf
Ha-shi -

For I have given you good instruction;
do not abandon My Torah.

כִּי לֶקַח טוֹב נָתַתִּי לָכֶם,
תּוֹרָתִי אַל תַּעֲזֹבוּ.

It it is a Tree of Life for those who hold fast to it,
and all its supporters are happy.
Its ways are ways of pleasantness,
and all its paths are peace.

עֵץ חַיִּים הִיא לַמַּחֲזִיקִים בָּהּ,
וְתֹמְכֶיהָ מְאֻשָּׁר.
דְּרָכֶיהָ דַרְכֵי נֹעַם,
וְכָל נְתִיבוֹתֶיהָ שָׁלוֹם.

Return us to You, Adonai, and we will return;
renew our days as of old.

הֲשִׁיבֵנוּ, יְיָ, אֵלֶיךָ וְנָשׁוּבָה,
חַדֵּשׁ יָמֵינוּ כְּקֶדֶם.

Lo Yarei-u

לא ירעו

Music: **Eliyahu Schleifer**, arr. **Anastasia Sobolev**
Text: Isaiah 11:9; Micah 4:4 / Torah service (Reform)

A Em Am/E Em/B G E7
a - - retz dei - ah et A - do - nai ka - ma - yim, ka -
p
Am Em Bm7 Em B7
mf
D.S. al Coda
ma - yim la - yam m'-cha - sim.
D.S. al Coda
CODA
Em SOLO N.C. Em7 A
mf
shi. V' - ya - sh'- vu ish ta - chat gaf - no v' -
mp

They shall not hurt or destroy in My holy mountain,
for the earth shall be filled with the knowledge of Adonai
as the sea-bed is covered by water.
And all shall sit under their vines and fig trees,
and none shall make them afraid.

לֹא־יָרֵעוּ וְלֹא־יַשְׁחִיתוּ
בְּכָל־הַר קָדְשִׁי כִּי־מָלְאָה הָאָרֶץ
דֵּעָה אֶת־יְיָ כַּמַּיִם לַיָּם מְכַסִּים.
וְיָשְׁבוּ אִישׁ תַּחַת גַּפְנוֹ
וְתַחַת תְּאֵנָתוֹ וְאֵין מַחֲרִיד.

Lamdeini Elohai

למדני אלוהי

Music: **Eliyahu Schleifer**, arr. **Raymond Goldstein**
Text: Leah Goldberg

C7 F Gm
13
ha - chei-rut ha - zot, lir - ot, la-chush, lin - shom, la -
C Dm B♭maj7 Dm
17
mf
dim.
da - at, l' - ya - cheil, l' - hi - ka - sheil.
p
B♭maj7 Am7 Dm B Dm G(sus4)/D G/D B♭maj9 Am7 Dm
21
mp
La - meid et sif - to - tai b'ra - chah v'-shir ha - leil, b' -
p

27
Dm C7 B♭maj7 F
cresc.
hit - cha-deish z'man - cha im bo - ker v'-im leil, l' - val yih'-yeh yo-
mf mp
32
C°/D Gm B♭7 mf Am Dm
mi ha - yom kit-mot shil- shom, l' - val yih'-yeh a - lai yo -
mf
Ped.
Ped.
37
B♭maj7 C Dm C Dm Gm Gm7 A7
dim.
mi her - geil.

Teach me, O God, a blessing, a prayer
on the mystery of a withered leaf,
on ripened fruit so fair,
on the freedom
to see, to sense, to breathe,
to know, to hope, to despair.

Teach my lips a blessing,
a hymn of praise,
as each morning
and night
You renew Your days,
lest my day today be as the one before;
lest routine set my ways.

לַמְּדֵנִי, אֱלֹהַי, בָּרֵךְ וְהִתְפַּלֵּל
עַל סוֹד עָלֶה קָמֵל,
עַל נֹגַהּ פְּרִי בָּשֵׁל,
עַל הַחֵרוּת הַזֹּאת:
לִרְאוֹת, לָחוּשׁ, לִנְשֹׁם,
לָדַעַת, לְיַחֵל, לְהִכָּשֵׁל.

לַמֵּד אֶת שִׂפְתוֹתַי
בְּרָכָה וְשִׁיר הַלֵּל,
בְּהִתְחַדֵּשׁ זְמַנְּךָ
עִם בֹּקֶר וְעִם לֵיל,
לְבַל יִהְיֶה יוֹמִי הַיּוֹם
כִּתְמוֹל שִׁלְשׁוֹם,
לְבַל יִהְיֶה עָלַי יוֹמִי הֶרְגֵּל.

Mah Tovu

מה טובו

Music: **Eliyahu Schleifer**, arr. **Anastasia Sobolev**
Text: Morning liturgy

Em Am/E Em Last time to Coda C Bm Am/E Em To Verses (solo)
mish - k'-no - te - cha, Yis - - ra - el!
Last time to Coda
To Verses
VERSE 1
Em C Bm/E
Va - a - ni b'-rov chas-d'-cha a - vo vei-te -
Am C7 Am Em Bm F♯m
cha, esh-ta-cha-veh el hei - chal kod-sh'-cha b'-yir - a - te -
VERSE 2
B Am D.S. Em Am D7
cha. A - do-nai, a - hav-ti m'-on bei - te - cha u-m-
D.S.

31
G A7/G B Am D7 G
mp
kom mish-kan k'-vo - de - cha. Va - a - ni esh - ta - cha - veh v'- ech -
35
Am Em B7 Em Am D7 G
mf
ra - ah, ev - r'-chah lif - nei A - do - nai o - si. Va - a -
40
Em A D/F♯ D7/F♯ G6 A♯o B B7
mp
f
ni t'- fi - la - ti l'- cha, A - do - nai, eit ra - tzon. E - lo -
44
Em7 C7 B7(omit3) G D B(sus4) B Em D9/E
him b'- rov chas - de - cha, a - nei - ni be - e - met yish - e - cha.
D.S. al Coda

𝄌 CODA

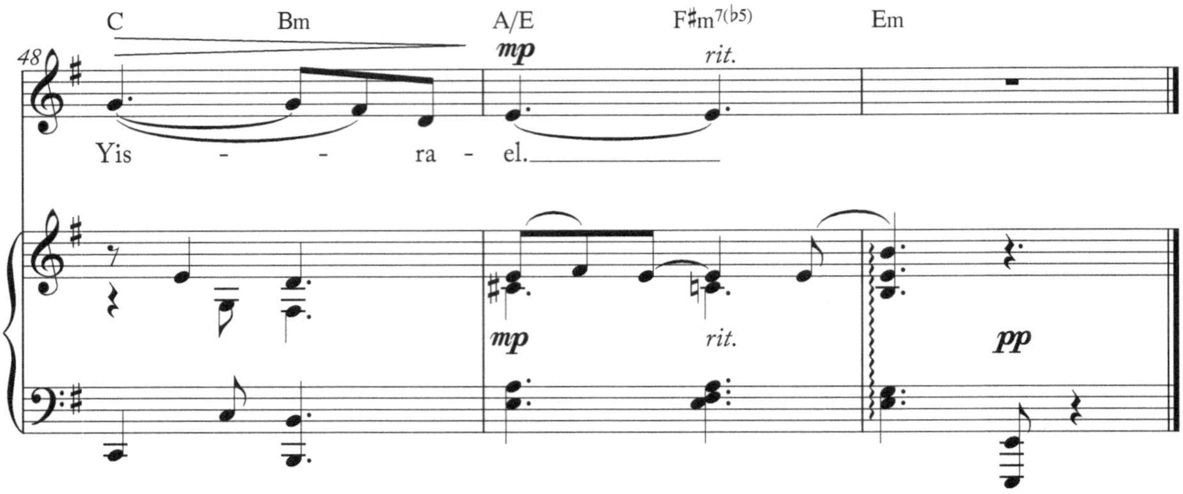

How fair are your tents, O Jacob,
your dwellings, O Israel.

מַה־טֹּבוּ אֹהָלֶיךָ, יַעֲקֹב,
מִשְׁכְּנֹתֶיךָ, יִשְׂרָאֵל!

I, through Your abundant love,
enter Your house;
I bow down in awe
at Your holy temple.

וַאֲנִי בְּרֹב חַסְדְּךָ
אָבוֹא בֵיתֶךָ,
אֶשְׁתַּחֲוֶה אֶל־הֵיכַל קָדְשְׁךָ
בְּיִרְאָתֶךָ.

Adonai, I love Your temple abode,
the dwelling-place of Your glory.

יְיָ, אָהַבְתִּי מְעוֹן בֵּיתֶךָ
וּמְקוֹם מִשְׁכַּן כְּבוֹדֶךָ.

I will humbly bow down low
before Adonai, my Maker.

וַאֲנִי אֶשְׁתַּחֲוֶה וְאֶכְרָעָה,
אֶבְרְכָה לִפְנֵי־יְיָ עֹשִׂי.

As for me, may my prayer come to You, Adonai,
at a favorable time.
O God, in Your abundant faithfulness,
answer me with Your sure deliverance.

וַאֲנִי תְפִלָּתִי לְךָ, יְיָ,
עֵת רָצוֹן.
אֱלֹהִים, בְּרָב־חַסְדֶּךָ,
עֲנֵנִי בֶּאֱמֶת יִשְׁעֶךָ.

Mah Nomar L'fanecha

מה נאמר לפניך

Music: **Eliyahu Schleifer**, arr. **Doron Schleifer**
Text: High Holy Day liturgy

Last time to Coda
B
a tempo
dei - a. A - tah yo - dei - a ra - zei o - lam; v' - ta - a - lu - mot sit -
rei kol chai. A - tah cho - feis kol chad - rei va - ten; u - vo -
chein k' - la - yot va - leiv. Ein da - var ne - e -
lam mi - me - ka; v' - ein nis - tar mi - ne - ged ei - ne - cha.
mf
mp

CODA

What can we say unto You
who dwells on high?
And what can we tell You
whose abode is beyond the heaven itself?

You certainly know everything revealed or hidden.
You know all the mysteries of the universe
and the dark secrets of all living souls.
You search the most hidden chambers of our conscience,
and You probe our hearts.
Nothing escapes You and nothing is hidden from Your sight.
English translation by Eliyahu Schleifer

מַה נֹּאמַר לְפָנֶיךָ, יוֹשֵׁב מָרוֹם,
וּמַה נְּסַפֵּר לְפָנֶיךָ, שׁוֹכֵן שְׁחָקִים.
הֲלֹא כָּל הַנִּסְתָּרוֹת
וְהַנִּגְלוֹת אַתָּה יוֹדֵעַ.

אַתָּה יוֹדֵעַ רָזֵי עוֹלָם,
וְתַעֲלוּמוֹת סִתְרֵי חָי.
אַתָּה חוֹפֵשׂ כָּל־חַדְרֵי־בָטֶן,
וּבוֹחֵן כְּלָיוֹת וָלֵב.
אֵין דָּבָר נֶעְלָם מִמֶּךָּ,
וְאֵין נִסְתָּר מִנֶּגֶד עֵינֶיךָ.

Modeh / Modah Ani מודה אני

Music: **Eliyahu Schleifer**, arr. **Anastasia Sobolev**
Text: Morning liturgy

Dedicated to Cantor Evan Cohen

B
Dm
Gm
Dm
13
deh a-ni l'-fa-ne-cha, Me-lech chai v'-ka-yam. Mo-
R.H.
17
Gm
Dm
dah a-ni l'-fa-ne-cha, Me-lech chai v'-ka-yam, she-he-che-
F/C C7 F N.C. Dm C7 F
21
rit.
a tempo
zar-ta bi nish-ma-ti b'-chem-lah, ra-bah e-mu-na-te-cha, she-he-che-

I offer thanks to You,
ever-living Sovereign,
that You have restored my soul to me in mercy:
How great is Your trust.

מוֹדֶה / מוֹדָה אֲנִי לְפָנֶיךָ,
מֶלֶךְ חַי וְקַיָּם,
שֶׁהֶחֱזַרְתָּ בִּי נִשְׁמָתִי בְּחֶמְלָה,
רַבָּה אֱמוּנָתֶךָ.

Mi Chamochah

מי כמוכה

Music: **Eliyahu Schleifer**, arr. **Anastasia Sobolev**
Text: Morning liturgy

Cm Cm/D D
mp
ra t'-hi-lot, o - - seih fe - le, no -
D Cm D Am7(♭5) D
mf mp
ra t'-hi-lot o - seih fe - le! Shi -
B
G C/G G C/G G C/G G C/G
f
rah cha-da-shah shi-b'-chu g'-u-lim, shi-b'-chu g'-u-lim l'-shim - cha al s'-
C/D D C D Em D N.C. G Em7
cresc.
f
fat ha-yam. Ya - chad ku - lam ho-du v'-him - li - chu, v'-him-

Who is like You, O God, among the gods that are worshiped?
Who is like You, majestic in holiness,
awesome in splendor, working wonders?

מִי כָמֹכָה בָּאֵלִם, יְיָ!
מִי כָּמֹכָה נֶאְדָּר בַּקֹּדֶשׁ,
נוֹרָא תְהִלֹּת, עֹשֵׂה פֶלֶא!

With new song, inspired, at the shore of the Sea, the redeemed sang Your praise.
In unison they all offered thanks.
Acknowledging Your sovereignty, they said:
"Adonai will reign forever!"

שִׁירָה חֲדָשָׁה שִׁבְּחוּ גְאוּלִים
לְשִׁמְךָ עַל שְׂפַת הַיָּם.
יַחַד כֻּלָּם הוֹדוּ וְהִמְלִיכוּ וְאָמְרוּ:
יְיָ יִמְלֹךְ לְעֹלָם וָעֶד.

K'dushah

קדושה

Music: **Eliyahu Schleifer**
Text: Shabbat morning liturgy

Let us sanctify Your name on earth,
as it is sanctified in the heavens above.
As it is written
by Your prophet:

נְקַדֵּשׁ אֶת שִׁמְךָ בָּעוֹלָם,
כְּשֵׁם שֶׁמַּקְדִּישִׁים אוֹתוֹ בִּשְׁמֵי מָרוֹם,
כַּכָּתוּב עַל יַד נְבִיאֶךָ,
וְקָרָא זֶה אֶל זֶה וְאָמַר:

Holy, holy, holy is *Adonai Tz'vaot!*
God's presence fills the whole earth.

קָדוֹשׁ, קָדוֹשׁ, קָדוֹשׁ יְיָ צְבָאוֹת,
מְלֹא כָל הָאָרֶץ כְּבוֹדוֹ.

Source of our strength, Sovereign One,
how majestic is Your presence in all the earth!

אַדִּיר אַדִּירֵנוּ, יְיָ אֲדֹנֵנוּ,
מָה אַדִּיר שִׁמְךָ בְּכָל הָאָרֶץ.

Blessed is the presence of God, shining forth from where God dwells.

בָּרוּךְ כְּבוֹד יְיָ מִמְּקוֹמוֹ.

God alone is our God and our Creator,
our Ruler and our Helper;
and in mercy, God is revealed in the sight of all the living:
I am Adonai your God!

אֶחָד הוּא אֱלֹהֵינוּ, הוּא אָבִינוּ,
הוּא מַלְכֵּנוּ, הוּא מוֹשִׁיעֵנוּ,
וְהוּא יַשְׁמִיעֵנוּ בְּרַחֲמָיו לְעֵינֵי כָּל חָי:
אֲנִי יְיָ אֱלֹהֵיכֶם.

Adonai shall reign forever, your God, O Zion,
from generation to generation, Hallelujah!

יִמְלֹךְ יְיָ לְעוֹלָם, אֱלֹהַיִךְ, צִיּוֹן,
לְדֹר וָדֹר, הַלְלוּיָהּ.

R'tzeih

רצה

Music: **Eliyahu Schleifer,** according to Shabbat morning *nusach;* arr. **Raymond Goldstein**
Text: From the *Amidah*

For Doron Schleifer

11
me - cha.
Eil ka -
mf
f
B
14
rov l'-chol ko-r-av, p'-neih el a-va-de-cha v'-cho-nei-nu, sh'-
17
foch ru-cha-cha a-lei-nu. V'-
rit.
rit.
C Moderato
20
p
te - che-ze-nah ei - nei-nu b'-shu - v'-cha l'-Tzi - yon, v'-
p

24
te - che-ze - nah_ ei - nei - nu b'-shu - v'-cha l'-Tzi - yon, v'-
28
mf
te - che-ze - nah ei - nei - nu b'-shu - v'-cha l'-Tzi-
mf
31
yon, v'- te - che-ze - nah_ ei - nei - nu b'-
34
mf rit.
shu - v'-cha l'-Tzi - yon, b'-ra - cha-mim._ Ba-
mp
rit.

Find favor, Adonai our God, with Your people Israel,
and accept their prayer with love.
May the worship of Your people Israel
always be acceptable.
God who is near to all who call,
turning lovingly to Your servants.
Pour out Your spirit upon us.

Let our eyes behold
Your loving return to Zion.

Blessed are You, Adonai,
whose Divine Presence returns to Zion.

רְצֵה, יְיָ אֱלֹהֵינוּ, בְּעַמְּךָ יִשְׂרָאֵל,
וּתְפִלָּתָם בְּאַהֲבָה תְקַבֵּל,
וּתְהִי לְרָצוֹן תָּמִיד
עֲבוֹדַת יִשְׂרָאֵל עַמֶּךָ.
אֵל קָרוֹב לְכָל קֹרְאָיו,
פְּנֵה אֶל עֲבָדֶיךָ וְחָנֵּנוּ,
שְׁפוֹךְ רוּחֲךָ עָלֵינוּ.

וְתֶחֱזֶינָה עֵינֵינוּ בְּשׁוּבְךָ
לְצִיּוֹן בְּרַחֲמִים.

בָּרוּךְ אַתָּה, יְיָ,
הַמַּחֲזִיר שְׁכִינָתוֹ לְצִיּוֹן.

Shehu Noteh Shamayim שהוא נוטה שמים

Music: **Eliyahu Schleifer**
Text: Liturgy ("Aleinu L'shabei-ach")

For You spread out the heavens and established the earth;
Your majestic abode is in the heavens above,
and Your mighty Presence is in the loftiest heights.
You are our God, and there is none else.
In truth You are our Sovereign without compare,
as is written in Your Torah: Know then this day
and take it to heart
that Adonai is surely God
in the heavens above
and on the earth below. There is none else.

שֶׁהוּא נוֹטֶה שָׁמַיִם וְיֹסֵד אָרֶץ,
וּמוֹשַׁב יְקָרוֹ בַּשָּׁמַיִם מִמַּעַל,
וּשְׁכִינַת עֻזּוֹ בְּגָבְהֵי מְרוֹמִים.
הוּא אֱלֹהֵינוּ, אֵין עוֹד,
אֱמֶת מַלְכֵּנוּ אֶפֶס זוּלָתוֹ.
כַּכָּתוּב בְּתוֹרָתוֹ: וְיָדַעְתָּ הַיּוֹם
וַהֲשֵׁבֹתָ אֶל לְבָבֶךָ,
כִּי יְיָ הוּא הָאֱלֹהִים
בַּשָּׁמַיִם מִמַּעַל
וְעַל הָאָרֶץ מִתָּחַת, אֵין עוֹד.

Shehashalom Shelo

שהשלום שלו

Music: **Eliyahu Schleifer**
Text: Shabbat *z'mirah* "Baruch Adonai Yom Yom"

For Lauren Bandman

May the Owner of peace
grant us blessing and peace.
May the Merciful One bless God's people with peace.

שֶׁהַשָּׁלוֹם שֶׁלּוֹ
יָשִׂים עָלֵינוּ בְּרָכָה וְשָׁלוֹם.
הָרַחֲמָן הוּא יְבָרֵךְ אֶת עַמּוֹ בַּשָּׁלוֹם.